# TROOP COMMITTEE GUIDEBOOK

BOY SCOUTS OF AMERICA

# CONTENTS

# FOREWORD

Character development, citizenship training, and personal fitness are the aims of Boy Scouting. These aims are achieved in a Boy Scout troop through the use of eight methods: The Ideals of Scouting, The Patrol Method, Advancement, Uniform, Outdoors, Leadership Development, Adult Male Association, and Personal Growth.

The Boy Scouts of America charters a community-based organization to operate a Boy Scout troop as a service to youth and to help meet the organization's own youth objectives.

The Scouting coordinator and troop committee are appointed by the head of the chartered organization to guarantee the achievement of its objectives and to support the effective operation of the troop. The troop committee has two primary responsibilities:

**1.** Recommend to the head of the chartered organization the best possible person to serve as Scoutmaster.

**2.** Help the Scoutmaster carry out good troop program.

Troop committee work is both interesting and challenging. You have an opportunity to help boys grow up in so many ways. The ideals of the Scout Oath and Law, "Do a Good Turn Daily," and "Be Prepared," together with the skills and other methods learned as a Scout, help a boy meet the challenges of today and prepare for tomorrow. In helping boys grow into useful citizens, you perform a valuable service to the community.

Dividends may not come to you immediately, but they will surely come as today's generation gently grasps the reins of leadership from you as time marches on.

## WHO Am I in Scouting?

I am a member of the troop committee of

Troop No. _____ , _____

Chartered to: _____

which meets monthly at _____

Day: _____ Time: _____

As a member of the troop committee I signed an Application for Charter for my troop on behalf of my chartered organization, in which I agreed, along with the others who signed the application, to do certain things. Those responsibilities appear on the application as follows:

# Chapter 1

# THE TROOP COMMITTEE

## TROOP COMMITTEE RESPONSIBILITIES

- Provide adequate meeting facilities.

- Advise Scoutmaster on policies relating to the Boy Scout program and the chartered organization.

- Carry out the policies and regulations of the Boy Scouts of America.

- Encourage leaders in carrying out the Boy Scout program.

- Be responsible for finances, adequate funds, and disbursements in line with the approved budget plan.

- Obtain, maintain, and care properly for troop property.

- Provide adequate camping and outdoor program (minimum 10 days and nights per year).

- See that adult leadership is assigned in case Scoutmaster is absent or is unable to serve.

- Operate troop to ensure permanency.

# Why a Troop Committee?

Troop committee work is both interesting and challenging. You make a significant contribution in helping boys grow up. The ideals of the Scout Oath and Law, together with the skills and methods a boy learns as a Scout, help him meet tomorrow's challenges—and today's. In helping boys grow into useful citizens you perform a valuable service to the community.

## Committee Functions

The elected boy leaders, known as the patrol leaders' council, working under the guidance of the Scoutmaster, are responsible for the troop program. This includes planning and carrying out troop meetings and outdoor programs.

Supporting the Scoutmaster with whatever assistance needed for the troop program is one of the chief responsibilities of the committee. The other is administration.

## Fulfilling Functions

To fulfill its responsibilities, the troop committee operates with each member having a responsibility—Membership/Relationships, Outdoor/Activities, Health and Safety, Finance/Records, Advancement, and so on—or it may operate as a committee of the whole. On a large troop committee, you might be one of three or four members in a group such as advancement or outdoor.

How the troop committee is structured is explained in the next chapter.

Chapter 2

# COMMITTEE
# OPERATIONS

The troop committee represents and is responsible to the chartered organization (sponsor). Usually the organization is a church or synagogue, school, PTA, service club, industry, or other formal organization. But sometimes it may be a group of citizens without other organizational ties. Here are the alternatives.

- An organization or group of citizens organizes a troop and provides a meeting place and adult leadership. Each troop has a separate troop committee.

- An organization operates two or more troops, packs, teams, or posts. There may be one troop committee serving all troops. Or a single committee may serve all troops, packs, teams, and posts.

- Two or more organizations may jointly operate one or more troops.

These alternatives for organizing a troop and committee operation make it possible to bring Scouting to any type of community. Obviously, how your committee functions depends in part on your own situation. What follows is the recommended procedure for a committee serving one or more Boy Scout troops.

It is important that a committee be organized at the same time a new Boy Scout troop is formed. New committee members should be added to an existing unit to replace those who drop out, lose interest, or have a change of available time.

# Committee Size and Organization

Experience has shown that troops with committees of seven or more members are stronger, have better program, and last longer. The minimum number of members is three adults, 21 years of age or older. Both men and women may be members. The logical place to look for new committee members is among the parents of Boy Scouts in the troop, members of the chartered organization, and other persons interested in youth. Regularly interview parents of new boys for committee members.

It is desirable that some troop committee members also be members of the chartered organization. They should also be interested in youth and be willing to devote the time that troop committee work requires. And it is only fair to troop committee members to tell them what that time commitment will be.

# Program Assistance

## Program Development

Program development is the task of the Scoutmaster. He or she is not formally a member of the committee, but assists the chairman in planning the agenda and attends troop committee meetings. The Scoutmaster presents the plans and needs of the troop program and assists the committee in its organizing to make the program happen.

The planning and conducting of troop meetings and other activities should be left to the patrol leaders' council, made up entirely of Scouts, with guidance and counsel from the Scoutmaster. The troop committee must give its approval to these plans and may, of course, make suggestions about them.

# Program Planning

Planning starts with consideration of program ideas from the troop. To learn what the Scouts themselves want, the patrol leaders are asked to get their members' preferences at a patrol meeting. The patrol members list their ideas, and lists are gathered and tallied at the planning conference of the patrol leaders' council.

The program, developed by the patrol leaders' council, goes to the troop committee for final approval. You should consider where you, as a member of the committee, can help in the various parts of the program.

Next, the program is presented to the parents and Scouts, preferably in a reproduced form they may keep for future reference.

At times it may be advisable to hold a split meeting, with adults giving consideration to policies and procedures while the boys meet in a separate part of the building to discuss plans on a boy-to-boy basis. A suggested agenda for this parents' meeting is on page 13.

Your committee should present a copy of the troop program to the Scouting coordinator with a copy for the head of the chartered organization (sponsor) and the unit commissioner.

# The Monthly Troop Program

With the plans made at the long-range program planning conference as a base, the patrol leaders' council meets once a month to make detailed plans for the next month's troop program and project for two more.

This is done entirely by the patrol leaders' council with the Scoutmaster's guidance. However, when the monthly plan has been drawn up, the program is presented to the troop committee by the Scoutmaster or by the senior patrol leader upon invitation of the committee. A discussion of these plans and the determination of support you can provide usually make up a major portion of your work at your monthly meeting. All members of the committee have jobs to do.

## Troop Meetings and Special Activities

Troop committee members do not attend the weekly troop meetings on a regular basis but are requested to help from time to time. Troop meetings are under the direction of the senior patrol leader, his staff, and the patrol leaders' council.

You will be called upon to assist in activities. For example, the special activity for an aquatic skills program feature might be a swimming meeting. The Scoutmaster might request your help in conducting that.

# PARENTS' NIGHT

## OPENING CEREMONY—5 minutes

Scout Oath and Law                    Patrol Leader

## PRESENTATION—30 minutes

Troop's tentative plans for the long-range program are outlined by the senior patrol leader. Slides of council summer camp or troop summer activities shown by the Order of the Arrow.

## SPLIT MEETING—30 minutes

### ADULTS

Distribution of the long-range program

Explanation of program features by troop committee member

Explanation and assigning of responsibilities

### BOYS

Discussion of troop's camping plans by troop leader

Games or special work on advancement

## CLOSING—10 minutes

Awards: Scouter's Wife Award, No. 3766

Scouter's Husband Award, No. 3765

Commendation to Chartered Organization, No. 3714

Appreciation certificates, No. 3722

Scoutmaster's Minute:

Ceremony:

# Chapter 3

# COMMITTEE CHAIRMAN

As chairman, you run the regular monthly meetings of the committee and work with the Scoutmaster in preparing the order of business for these meetings. You are responsible for seeing that the committee functions and that the work is coordinated and completed. In addition, you must be available to advise and assist committee members.

You will work closely with the Scouting coordinator in discharging the following duties:

- Organize the committee to see that all functions are delegated, coordinated, and completed.

- Assist in the recruitment of the best individuals available for Scoutmaster and assistants.

- Maintain a close relationship with the Scouting coordinator.

- Interpret national and local council policies to the troop.

- Work closely with the Scoutmaster in preparation of agenda for troop committee meeting.

- Call, preside, and promote attendance at monthly troop committee meetings and any special meetings that may be called.

- Ensure troop representation at monthly roundtables.

- Secure topflight, trained people for camp leadership.

- Arrange for charter review and recharter the troop annually.

# Committee Assignments

The areas of the troop committee's responsibilities are explained in the following chapters. These must be divided among the committee members.

If your committee has only three members, each member must be responsible for two or more of these areas. On the other hand, if you have a troop committee with perhaps 15 members, two or three members would deal with each area or the responsibilities could be further divided to be shared among the individuals of a larger committee.

If the troop has only 10 or 12 Scouts, three or four committee members could handle the load. As the troop grows, however, so should the committee. A committee with only three or four active members will have its hands full giving the necessary support to a troop.

# Leadership

Perhaps the single most important responsibility of the chartered organization is recruiting and then supporting the adult leaders who work directly with the Scouts—your Scoutmaster and assistants. The Scoutmaster must be at least 21 years old and appointed by the head of the chartered organization upon the recommendation of the troop committee.

## Securing a Scoutmaster

**The Troop Committee's Most Important Job**

# SECURING A SCOUTMASTER ✠

### Six sure steps for success...

Your Scoutmaster works with patrol, troop, and Scouting coordinator to bring Scouting to your boys and must be 21 or over. The Scoutmaster will influence the life of every boy in the troop. The job calls for the best leader available.

A time-tested, six-step plan called Securing a Scoutmaster, No. 3072, has been developed to guide the chartered organization in recruiting a troop leader. This tested plan will produce a good Scoutmaster if it is followed carefully. By using the six steps, recruiters will avoid the gross errors of advertising for a leader, getting the head of the chartered organization to cry the blues and ask for volunteers at a public meeting, signing up an eager but incompetent person, or asking everyone and anyone in the hope that someone will accept. Any one of these can be fatal to a troop.

# Assistant Scoutmasters

Assistant Scoutmasters are important for two reasons. First, they provide the two-deep leadership that ensures continuous, effective management of your troop. If for some reason the Scoutmaster must be replaced, a trained leader who is already acquainted with the boys is available to step into the top spot. Secondly, they help relieve the load on the Scoutmaster. An assistant Scoutmaster is given specific responsibilities based on abilities, such as Activities, Physical Arrangements, or Patrol/Leadership Corps adviser. The assistant shares in planning, offers advice, and makes decisions.

The qualities to be sought in an assistant Scoutmaster are much the same as those required of the Scoutmaster. An assistant Scoutmaster may be as young as 18, but one assistant should be 21 years old or older to be able to replace the Scoutmaster if necessary.

Since the Scoutmaster works closely with the assistants, he or she appoints the assistant Scoutmasters with the approval of the troop committee. Work with the Scoutmaster on this matter. You can adapt a successful procedure for finding, selecting, and securing assistant Scoutmasters from the six steps in Securing a Scoutmaster.

# Adult Leader Training

To be effective, the person you select as Scoutmaster must become acquainted with the aims and methods of the Scouting movement and the methods Scouting uses to help in a boy's growth. Boy Scouting Fast Start videos, *Troop Organization, The Troop Meeting,* and *The Outdoor Program,* are designed to help you get started. These can be provided by your commissioner or an experienced Scouter. Contact your local council service center.

The Boy Scouts of America has developed a series of training experiences for your adult leaders—specifically the Scoutmaster—

from the time they accept the position. They are designed to prepare leaders to carry out their assigned jobs.

It is your responsibility to see that your Scoutmaster and assistants participate in these experiences.

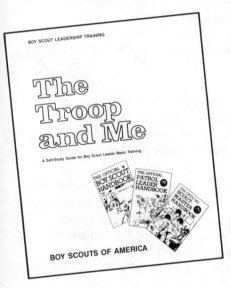

Your district offers training courses for new Scoutmasters, assistants, and troop committee members. Your commissioner or the council service center will have details. If there is not a course scheduled to take place soon, *The Troop and Me, A Self-Study Guide for Boy Scout Leader Basic Training,* No. 6554, and personal coaching is available from your commissioner or an experienced Scouter. They will help you to plan the program and train your boy leaders.

**Supplemental Adult Leader Training is available in these areas:** Skill Awards, The Advancement Plan, Scoutmaster Conference, Understanding Boy Scouts with Handicaps, and Counseling.

**Roundtables:** Districts throughout the country conduct regular Scout leaders' program meetings for all adult troop members. These meetings, usually called roundtables, emphasize troop program. Troop leaders pick up skills and games as well as songs, stunts, ceremonies, and ideas. Scoutmasters and troop committee members share successful solutions to situations they have in common. Many immediate helps for troop program are the result of roundtable participation. As a rule, roundtables are held monthly.

**Wood Badge** is the advanced training program for Boy Scout leaders. It is conducted in two phases. Phase I is a concentrated week or series of weekends of learning experiences within the structure of a patrol and troop in an outdoor setting. Phase II gives participants the opportunity to apply to their Scouting job what they have learned in phase I. The participant and a counselor evaluate the results. A maximum of 2 years is allowed on phase II. When this is satisfactorily completed, the participant is awarded the Wood Badge beads.

It is recommended that a Scoutmaster participate in phase I of Wood Badge within 2 years following completion of the initial Adult Leader Development.

**The Scouter's Key** is available to the Scoutmaster who successfully applies the techniques of Scouting and leadership skills. Requirements are available through your council service center.

# Providing Interim Leadership

If the Scoutmaster must be replaced, the assistant Scoutmaster who has been training as the understudy takes over. If circumstances find your troop without two-deep leadership, you and other troop committee members must make sure the troop keeps meeting until the right person can be secured as Scoutmaster. You must maintain your troop in that period at as high a level of performance as possible.

A similar problem is the need for members for the troop committee. When a troop committee is short of members, the rest of you must pick up functions of the missing people while you quickly seek replacements. The need or function to be filled should serve as the guide in the selection. This gives individuals the opportunity to work where they can make their best contribution.

# Monthly Troop Appraisal Sheet

### What is the appraisal sheet?

- It is a checklist—or reminder sheet—of most of the things that should be watched in a Boy Scout troop.

- It provides the troop committee, troop leader, and assistants, as well as the commissioner, with a comprehensive analysis of facts based on needs and progress of the troop.

- It is the medium through which the commissioner is able to provide vitally necessary factual information about the troop for follow-up.

### Why is it to be used monthly?

- A monthly checkup by all who are responsible for the success of the troop is the only way a continuity of effort and proper results can be assured.

- It is a reminder of what we need to be working on.

### Who does the appraising?

- The troop committee, troop leader, and assistants.

- As the appraisal is made the commissioner should be ready to answer any questions or be of whatever help possible.

# Troop Committee Meetings

Troop committee meetings should be held monthly. The best time is at the end of each month, after the patrol leaders' council plans the program for the month ahead.

The once-a-month meeting schedule has two advantages: (1) It keeps the committee aware of the troop's current program and what support is needed for it; and (2) it provides a regular opportunity for the committee to hold boards of review.

In addition to troop committee members, the Scoutmaster and assistant Scoutmasters normally attend the meetings. The Scouting coordinator and the commissioner should be invited to attend meetings periodically.

There will be times when you may want to hold your meetings outdoors, particularly if you are planning a special outdoor activity. In that case, why not meet at the site?

Discussion leads to understanding of goals and to action. But discussion must be directed to keep it from going in all directions. To prevent this, the chairman and the Scoutmaster should get together and prepare an order of business. The following is a suggested agenda that may be adapted to your committee's requirements. It represents a maximum agenda involving most of the committee's assignments and responsibilities.

## Suggested Order of Business
## Troop Committee Meeting

Call the meeting to order.
Welcome and Introductions (Scouting coordinator and/or commissioner)

Reading and action on minutes of the previous meeting.

Reports:

• Scoutmaster (troop progress, patrol leaders' council program, disciplinary problems, irregular attendance, outdoor experiences planned, other needs of the troop)

• Membership/Relationships (boys joining and leaving, parent orientation, recruiting plans, Webelos Scout graduation, newsletter, resource survey)

• Outdoor/Activities (outdoor and special activities, camp log progress, troop equipment, district and council activities)

• Health and Safety (tour permits, site inspection, safety training opportunities)

- Finance/Records (budget standing, money-earning projects, camp savings plan, sustaining membership enrollment)

- Advancement (boards of review, courts of honor, merit badge counselor list, Scouts advancing and those who are not)

- Service/Good Turn (advancement projects, service projects, service to chartered organization)

- Chairman (review priorities requiring attention)

Old business and new business are taken up in order.

Announcements (date of next month's troop committee meeting)

Adjourn.

# Priorities

| ____ Acceptable | ____ Requires Attention |
|---|---|
| September | March |
| October | April |
| November | May |
| December | June |
| January | July |
| February | August |

**Operation**

Seven Committee Members Assigned*

Committee Meets Monthly* (at least 9 times a year)

Monthly Boards of Review*
   PLC:                              TC:

Parent Orientation for New Scout Families

Troop Newsletter

Budget Plan* (Include *Boys' Life*)

Membership Plan
Long-Term Camp Plans*

Courts of Honor* Quarterly

Parents' Nights Quarterly

## Leadership

Scoutmaster Appointed by Head Chartered Organization*

Scoutmaster Completed Scoutmastership Fundamentals*

Two Assistant Scoutmasters (One over 21 years old)*

Assistant Scoutmasters Completed Scoutmastership Fundamentals

Roundtable Attended (at least one troop leader)

Leaders Wear Uniform

Patrol Leaders' Council operates Troop

Troop (or Patrol) Meeting (or Activity) Held Weekly

Junior Leader Training

Annual/Monthly Program Planning

## Support

10 Days and Nights Camping*

Scouts in Troop* 40% First Class or Higher

Intertroop Activity

Troop and Patrol Service Projects

Scouts Wear Uniform

*Supports one of the Quality Troop items.*

# The Chairman's Relationships

**With Chartered Organization.** The troop committee is appointed by the organization to operate the troop. Thus, your committee is directly responsible to it for making sure that the Scouting program is being offered. Your liaison with the organization is through your Scouting coordinator.

**With Scouting Coordinator.** You as the committee chairman deal with this person whenever questions of policy arise. Some of the ways the Scouting coordinator can help you and the troop committee are:

- Serves as head of "Scouting Department."

- Secures committee chairman and encourages training.

- Maintains a close liaison with troop committee chairman.

- Helps recruit the right leadership.

- Serves as liaison between the units and the organization.

- Organizes enough units.

- Encourages graduation of youth members from unit to unit.

- Assists with unit rechartering.

- Encourages service to organization.

- Cultivates organization leaders.

- Is an active and involved member of the district committee.

- Brings district help and promotes its use.

- Is a member of the local council representing the interests of the organization.

**With the Scoutmaster.** Your relations with the Scoutmaster should be cooperative, supportive, and supervisory. The Scoutmaster devotes much time and energy to your troop. The appreciation of enthusiastic Scouts may be expressed, but, rewarding as this is, leaders need the appreciation of adults, too. A Scoutmaster who does a good job should be told about it. Praise all your leaders in public—at courts of honor, meetings of the chartered organization, and parents' nights.

Occasional token gifts showing the troop's appreciation are appropriate. A simple piece of camping equipment or an engraved miniature Scout statuette are acceptable gifts.

**With Patrol Leaders' Council.** The troop committee has no direct relationships with the patrol leaders' council. This council is made up of the senior patrol leader, patrol leaders, and a representative of the leadership corps. It is the program planning body for the troop. Your relationship with the patrol leaders' council will be through the Scoutmaster.

**With Parents of Scouts.** Parents, with the best reason in the world to be interested in troop affairs, may not want to interfere. Troop committee members and the Scoutmaster must take the initiative in explaining to parents their privileges and obligations. Parents' orientation meetings, parents' meetings, troop activities, and courts of honor present good opportunities for this.

Tell them how the troop operates, the time meetings start and finish, how their son earns ranks, and what he does as a Scout. Give them firsthand information about the troop's financial operation.

Parents' meetings should be held quarterly, or at least twice a year.

Parents should be told about how the council is financed including support from the United Way and sustaining memberships. Parents normally will be given a chance to become a sustaining member each year.

**With the Commissioner.** The commissioner is a volunteer representative of the local council who helps by visiting troop and troop committee meetings to learn of needs. Get acquainted with and invite the commissioner to committee meetings.

The commissioner can advise on selecting a leader and will assist with the annual rechartering by reviewing the troop's performance with adult leaders. The commissioner can assist in any program planning problems. This person's ability to solve problems or to secure the help to solve them is important.

When there are circumstances that prevent the service of a commissioner, and problems develop, your Scouting coordinator should present the troop's needs to the district committee.

# Facilities

The facilities function includes responsibility for the troop's regular meeting place.

# The Meeting Place

Your troop's home is its meeting place; part of your job is to be responsible for facilities needed for meetings. You have a real opportunity to ensure the success of the program through three simple considerations:

- **Area.** Consider the needs—the number of boys, activities, and equipment. Low ceilings, for instance, hamper some activities.

- **Availability.** The room must be available the same day and time each week.

- **Atmosphere.** Scouts should have an opportunity to decorate the room with charts, banners, and flags to give the room a Scouting atmosphere. Each patrol needs a corner to develop. The atmosphere helps put across the ideals of Scouting.

If you are unable to leave your Scouting displays on the walls from one meeting to the next, a troop equipment storage locker is a possible solution. A properly designed locker can provide for storing program equipment as well as portable screens for displaying the charts, trophies, and plaques that give flavor to the meeting place.

Periodically—once or twice a year—inspect the meeting place for health and safety hazards. A Meeting Place Inspection form, No. 6140, is available from your local council.

# Charter Renewal Procedures

No greater responsibility exists than to see that your troop continues to function year after year to provide a program for boys. A prompt and orderly registration procedure for your troop plus an efficient recruiting program are steps in achieving this objective.

# Plan

- **Three Months Before Troop Expiration.** The national office forwards to the local council a computer printout of adults and youth members presently registered. This form serves as the unit charter application and is inserted into the prepared unit charter renewal kit. The professional or commissioner serving the district delivers the kit to the key person in the chartered organization to carry out the steps of charter renewal.

- **Two Months Before Unit Expiration.** Using the computer printout, the unit conducts a membership inventory of youth and adults. It sets unit charter review date and invites officials of the chartered organization, the unit committee, unit leaders, and the unit commissioner or a district or council representative.

- **One Month Before Unit Expiration.** The unit commissioner, or a district or council representative, conducts the unit charter review. It includes a review of the unit's performance during the past year. The standard for the National Quality Unit Award is the basis for determining unit performance. Units are recognized for achieving this standard. The unit reregistration forms are completed and are submitted with fees to the council service center prior to the unit expiration date.

- **After the Charter Application Has Been Renewed.** The unit's new charter and membership certificates are presented to the chartered organization at an appropriate gathering. (Allow about 8 weeks from time unit is reregistered in council service center.)

# Rechartering and Review Meeting
## (Suggested Agenda)

- Review chartered organization's responsibility and the supporting services from the local council.

- Review the results of membership inventory and uniform inspection (from preprinted charter renewal).

- National Quality Unit commitments are reviewed to determine if troop achieves a Quality Unit status. Set objectives for the Quality Unit Award for the troop by using the commitment sheet, No. 14-222.

- Discuss council and district calendar of events.

- Explain budget plan and Unit Money-Earning Application and purpose.

- Review functions and assignments of troop committee members.

- Check for accuracy and completeness of renewal roster. Refer to No. 28-420B, "How to Fill Out the Unit Charter Renewal Application."

- Plan a charter presentation ceremony. (Allow 8 weeks.) Set date _____

- Set date to transmit the charter papers and fees to the council service center. Date _____

The charter presentation completes the annual registration procedure. This ceremony gives recognition to both boys and leaders and to your chartered organization. Your presentation ceremony can be formal or informal, but it should be serious and impressive.

This charter allows your boys to continue to be or become Scouts. As registered Scouts, they are permitted to wear the uniforms and distinctive badges of the program.

# Chapter 4

# MEMBERSHIP/ RELATIONSHIPS
## (Secretary)

Keeping the troop at full strength and involving parents and members of the chartered organization (sponsor) is very important to the success of Scouting. You will work closely with the committee chairman and the Scoutmaster in discharging the following duties:

- Keep minutes of meetings and send out committee meeting notices.

- Handle publicity.

- Conduct parent orientation for new families.

- Prepare family newsletter of troop events and activities.

- Work with troop historian.

- Assist in annual membership inventory and inspection program.

- Arrange for proper welcome of Webelos Scouts graduating into troop.

- Invite all Webelos Scout families to assist with troop program.

- Conduct boy-fact survey and troop resource survey.

- Plan for family night programs and family activities.

- See that the troop sets membership goals and adopts and carries out a troop recruiting plan.

- Plan charter presentation program.

As the secretary, you send notices of committee meetings and keep the minutes of these meetings. In addition, you are responsible for publicity. As publicist for the committee, your job is to report troop activities for the benefit of your chartered organization, community leaders, and prospective adult leaders as well as the general public. You provide news releases on all troop activities, including camping trips, courts of honor, special events, and elections or appointments of officers. Give these releases to your community newspapers, local radio and television stations, company publications, troop newsletter (if you have one), and the chartered organization's publication. Also, post news on the organization's bulletin board. Involve Scouts who are interested in journalism or photography to help you do the troop publicity job. The area of publicity is important—but all too often neglected.

## Membership

Your troop program must be interesting to hold boys—and a good program should attract more boys. Membership should not be left to chance, however. You should have new members coming in from your affiliated Cub Scout pack and other packs. Scouts can invite non-Scouts to join, and, at least once a year, you should conduct a membership roundup. Spring recruiting makes a lot of sense. Boys then become Scouts in time to get in on spring activities and summer camp. However, experience shows that monthly recruiting is best.

The simplest and most natural way for a boy to come into Scouting is through graduation from a Webelos den. If your chartered organization does not have a Cub Scout pack, seek out a pack with which you can cooperate. When a boy graduates as a Webelos Scout, your Scoutmaster and the boy's prospective patrol leader should attend the pack ceremony to receive the boy and his parents on behalf of the troop.

Don't forget the boys who dropped out of Cub Scouting. Many of these boys never become Scouts because they are never invited to join a patrol.

## Boy Scout Parent/Family Training

The training of parents is a constant process that should begin before or as soon as the family joins the troop and is best done in an informal setting. During a visit in the home, at a rally or School Night program, these things should be done:

- Review with the family the procedure for joining the troop, helping when asked in activities, dues, and the Boy Scout advancement plan.

- Review the parent authorization on the Boy Scout application.

- Review "Suggested Letter to Parents" on page 97.

- Review leaflet "What Parents Should Know About Our Scout Troop."

- Ask them to fill out a copy of the Parent-Interest Survey sheet.

- Make arrangements for the next step in family training, take part in Boy Scout Parent Orientation.

# Recruiting Plans

There are several proven methods to help troops conduct membership recruiting campaigns. Let's consider two major types.

**Troop Rally Night.** This is an open house for prospects and their parents to meet and visit with parents, leaders, and members of your troop to become acquainted with your activities and have the opportunity to join.

An organized campaign begins with your committee about 60 days before the rally night and involves the participation of the committee, adult leaders, parents of Scouts, patrol leaders' council, leadership corps, and patrols.

The plan includes the following steps:

- Take an inventory of your troop, showing the number of patrols and the number of boys. Determine the number of additional patrols you want and the number of boys needed to fill them. This provides you with an idea of the total number of boys you need to recruit.

- Conduct a boy-fact survey. You can gather information on potential Scouts by conducting a boy-fact survey. The district or council usually carries out most boy-fact surveys, but you can conduct your own within your chartered organization or at a neighborhood school. It's important, however, that approval be obtained from the district committee prior to contacting school officials to conduct a survey to establish a recruiting program within the schools. This is to avoid any previous commitment or agreement between the council and the school system.

When approval has been granted, a member of the troop committee or the Scouting coordinator may make arrangements with the principal of an elementary school in the neighborhood to conduct a survey.

Have every boy in the institution or school between the ages of 10 and 14 fill out a Boy-Fact Survey Card, No. 3712. Obtain information on 10-year-olds, too, even though they cannot join Scouting until after they have completed the fifth grade or have reached their 11th birthday or have completed the Arrow of Light Award. The survey card will provide you with such information as the boy's name and address, his age and date of birth, his parents or guardian, church or synagogue, school, and whether he is interested in becoming a Scout. This survey can give you a good picture of your recruiting possibilities.

- Evaluate the survey. Arrange these names according to streets where troop members live. In addition, organize the 10-year-olds by the month of the year they become 11 or graduate from the fifth grade.

- Make assignments of the names of boys who are eligible to join. Do this at a patrol leaders' meeting. Suggest to patrol leaders that boys should be invited to join as prospective patrol members. Keep a record of the name and address of each prospect and the name of the troop member assigned to invite him.

- Extend the invitation. About 2 weeks before the rally night, plan to return to the location where the survey was taken and hold a brief 10- or 15-minute session with the prospective members to capture their interest and to invite them to bring their parents to your Troop Rally Night at your regular meeting place. Distribute copies of Join the Scouts, No. 6526, with information on the date, time, and place of your rally night. If it is impossible to make a personal visit, send an invitation home by mail.

- Your Scouts follow up the invitations and call on individual prospects personally.

- Recruit family of your Scouts to telephone family of prospects several days ahead of the rally night to share their enthusiasm for Scouting and extend an additional invitation.

- At the rally night have a supply of Scout Applications and copies of What Parents Should Know About Our Scout Troop, No. 6511, available for distribution. During the program, a member of the committee should inform parents about your troop operation based on this leaflet. Follow through by having parents fill out the Troop Resource Survey, No. 4437, as an aid to recruiting their help at a later date.

- Following the rally night the committee should follow up on boys who did not come or did not sign up as Scouts.

- The new boys should be made welcome by troop members and leaders alike, and a Scout should be assigned to help the new member with his Tenderfoot rank requirements.

**School Night for Scouting.** Recruiting can be done through a program known as School Night for Scouting. The purpose of the program is to enroll new Cub Scouts and Boy Scouts in existing packs and troops, to enlist parent participation in the Scouting program, and to organize new units as necessary.

The program consists of one night when boys and parents are invited to special meetings in all the schools of an area. Organized by the council through school superintendents and principals, it includes parochial and private schools as well as public.

Troop leaders participate in School Night by preparing troop displays and by meeting with parents of potential Scouts. You play an important role in your troop's participation and should have an overall understanding of School Night for Scouting.

Perhaps the most important part of the program is the meeting held by the unit. You urge parents to "join" Scouting with their sons. You have a chance to give detailed information on your troop—its leadership, meeting time and place, registration fee, *Boys' Life,* and policies and procedures.

# Chapter 5

# OUTDOOR/ACTIVITIES

Camping and activities in the out-of-doors are what attracted boys to the Scouting program. You will work closely with the committee chairman and the Scoutmaster in carrying out the following:

- Supervise and help procure camp equipment.

- Work with Scoutmaster or assistant and quartermaster on inventory, storage, and proper maintenance of troop equipment.

- Help in securing permission to use camping sites.

- Serve as transportation coordinator.

- Encourage monthly outdoor activities or special activities.

- Promote National Camping Award and Fair Way camp promotion plan.

- Promote—through family meetings—attendance at troop camps, camporees, and summer Scout camp to reach the goal of 10 days and nights of camping for each Scout.

- Coordinate family camping program.

# Outdoor Program Support

Even when meeting indoors, Scouts focus their activities on preparation for the day when they will use their skills outdoors. The outdoor opportunity may be a day hike, a more ambitious overnight camp, or a long-term camp of a week or more during the summer or extended holiday.

Outdoor training, outdoor skills, and outdoor fun are important the year round, because these are activities the boys like and should have under proper adult leadership. Scouting's outdoor program is significant because it requires cooperation, the sharing of responsibility, and provides time for the practice of Scouting skills. The patrol method comes to life. Physical stamina, moral fiber, and spiritual understanding are enhanced by the outdoors. Life afield makes boys aware of some of the recreational opportunities to be found in the wilderness.

# Outdoors the Year Round

As troop outdoor plans are developed for the year, there are two objectives that every troop committee should provide:

**1.** At least 10 days and nights of camping for every Boy Scout in the troop

**2.** A long-term camp (6 or more consecutive days) for the entire troop membership

The outdoor program is planned as one of the major parts of the annual planning conference of the patrol leaders' council. Normally, the long-term camp is planned for the summer months at the established council camp, or a troop tour camp is organized.

The tentative program outlined by the boys and their leaders is presented to you and the troop committee for approval.

You have a number of responsibilities in this outdoor program:

• Make certain that leadership is provided for troop camping activities including at least two adults.

• Ensure adequate financing for the program.

• Provide for transportation and needed equipment.

• Inform parents of all the details, particularly about plans for both short- and long-term camping trips.

**Long-Term Camping.** Scout camping is troop camping—by patrols under troop leadership. The success of the program is measured by the extent to which the troop stands on its own feet, uses its boy leaders, trains its own instructors in various skills, and acquires new interests that may serve to stimulate the building of a camping program.

**Short-Term Camping—Hiking.** The biggest event of the year is the summer camp, but that is only part of troop camping. Overnight camps during the fall, winter, and spring, together with hikes in between, prepare for the summer. A good camping troop has as many as a dozen weekend and holiday camps during the year and also takes part in the district or council camporee. These overnights often add up to 12 nights and 24 days in camp—not counting overnight camps that individual patrols may take on their own. Since you are responsible for providing facilities and supervision for short-term camps, you should take part in troop activity planning from the start, make sure equipment is adequate, secure permission for use of campsites, and provide necessary transportation.

Scout camping is unique in these fundamental ways:

• The basic camping group, the patrol, is organized year round.

• The camp program is motivated and guided by adults but carried on by boys.

• Scout camping must include practices that result in personal fitness, self-reliance, individual initiative, cooperative outdoor living, spiritual awareness, and comparable attributes that contribute to good character and citizenship.

• Scout camping calls for two-boy tents, not the use of buildings.

• Equipment and provisions are carried to the site by boys backpacking on the trail.

• Meals and camping are by patrols and under patrol leadership, but always under the general supervision of trained adults.

**Kinds of Camps.** There are three types of arrangements you can make for your troop summer camp program.

1. Troop Camping on Council Property. Your troop camps on a site set apart for it at your local council camp. Your troop lives its own life under its own leadership, subject only to council regulations for the use of the campsite. The council often furnishes the tents, cooking gear, and other equipment. Sanitary arrangements, a tested water supply, and medical attention are taken care of by the council. Trained leaders supervise swimming and boating. Other experts are available to aid with Scout skills, nature lore, and other activities. A merit badge counseling program has been set up. Your troop also benefits from association with other troops, learning new methods and enjoying occasional large campfires together.

2. The Independent Camp. Your troop camps on a suitable campsite procured by itself and depends solely upon its own leadership to live up to council regulations and national camping standards. You receive only such help as your council may be able to give at long range. Your troop must provide its own camping gear from tentage to waterfront equipment and develop its own sanitary arrangements. It must test and treat its own water supply, develop safe swimming facilities, and secure trained waterfront aides. It must provide its own health supervision and medical examiner.

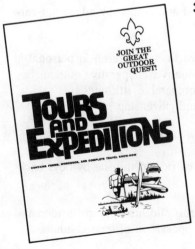

3. The Traveling Camp. Your troop arranges transportation and itinerary and is responsible for all food, shelter, and leadership.
Your troop travels from one interesting area to another with overnight camps at different locations throughout the trip. When planning a trip of this type, you should obtain *Campways Tours and Expeditions,* No. 3734, and study it carefully. The book is an invaluable guide to conducting a successful traveling camp.

# Recruiting Camp Leadership

Your troop committee must provide for the selection of responsible adult leadership, at least two adults who are 21 years of age, to give supervision to all troop camps. By far the best leader is the troop's Scoutmaster. This is so because:

- Your Scoutmaster knows each boy and his home background. The Scoutmaster also knows the personal problems each boy may have and is, therefore, better fitted to help him.

- Your Scoutmaster knows the ability of each boy in Scout skills and his leadership ability.

- When the Scoutmaster goes to camp, it rallies the interest of more boys.

- The Scoutmaster is known and trusted by the parents.

- The camp staff can serve the troop more effectively through the registered troop leader.

- Continuity of the program can be better carried out both before and after camping.

- Scoutmasters in camp share experiences with other leaders and see how other troops operate, thereby becoming more successful themselves.

- When troop leadership attends summer camp, it lessens the cost for each boy. This is possible because the expense of having the camp provide the direct leadership is avoided.

While it is most logical and desirable for the Scoutmaster to attend camp with the troop, it may happen that it is impossible for the Scoutmaster to go. If the problem is the Scoutmaster's work schedule, it may be possible to get extra vacation time if the proper approach is made to employer and/or union. This approach should be made only with the consent of the Scoutmaster.

If this cannot be worked out, then the troop committee must look elsewhere for camp leadership. You can recruit supplementary leadership from among the parents, troop committee, or members of the organization. You will find it more desirable, and often easier, to secure two leaders than one. These leaders must be willing to take some basic training and have an interest in the boys of the troop and their individual needs. Should all your efforts fail to secure camp leadership, call on your council for help.

Here are the steps you should take in selecting your camp leadership:

1. Your Scoutmaster should be your first choice.

2. In the event the Scoutmaster cannot attend camp, proceed to list the best qualified adults in order of desirability—from among the assistant Scoutmasters, troop committee, parents, and members of the chartered organization.

3. Appoint a two-member committee to call on the candidates, beginning with the top of the list. Explain the plan for camping, tell of committee and council help, emphasize the importance of camping to the boys in the troop, and request that the candidate be one of the camp leaders for the troop.

4. If your candidate needs time to consider the proposal, call back at the agreed-upon time to get an answer. Two to 6 days should be sufficient.

5. The same procedure is followed with the second and third candidates, and so on until two adult leaders are secured.

6. Your council service center should be notified of the selection so that your camp leadership can be invited to camp training sessions.

## Telling Your Camping Story

Your council will provide general information on camp for the parents and Scouts. But you and the rest of the troop committee must give parents full, detailed information about your troop plans.

You may have to do an all-out selling job with parents so that they not only endorse the camping program of the troop, but provide the help you may need with transportation and leadership.

A parents' night should be held in the early fall. The main purpose of this meeting is to share information and to gain general acceptance by parents, leaders, troop committee members, and boys of the full program of the troop in general. The dates and location of summer camp will probably be announced at this time.

You should hold a second meeting with parents in March or April aimed exclusively at camping. Your primary purpose should be to give a complete orientation on troop plans and arrangements for the long-term summer camp.

The preopening should include displays of camping equipment, camping skills, and different phases of outdoor activity.

The master of ceremonies should be your troop committee chairman. The chairman's opening remarks tell the purpose for the evening. Information about the dates for camp and camp leadership is announced.

Your report on outdoor program support should be of a positive nature. Give details of all that has been decided. Include dates, the camp selected, counseling services provided by the camp staff, plan for waterfront instruction and protection, and an explanation of dietary provisions (emphasize the inclusion of plenty of milk, fruits, and vegetables). Explain the health and safety plan, including such details as the camp physician, resident health administrator or nurse, health lodge, health and accident insurance coverage on campers, and arrangements for emergency treatment with a nearby hospital. Also tell about the physical setup of the camp, including the camping equipment available—tents and cots, the number of boys assigned to each tent, and how transportation will be provided.

The treasurer's report shows parents how they can finance the camping period. The treasurer should explain what the boys, what the troop, and what the council pays for. The camp savings plan should be explained.

The camp leader asks the cooperation of the parents ensuring camp attendance by every Scout. The leader explains how parents do their part, pointing out that the whole year's Scouting program is designed as preparation for the summer camp experience.

In addition to literature on the camp, each family should be given a camp reservation card to be returned as soon as possible to the treasurer with the reservation fee. You will then have the information you need to complete camping plans.

Parents should be encouraged to ask questions of individual troop committee members either during a brief period before the closing or during the refreshment period afterward.

As a follow-up to the parents' night, you and other troop committee members should visit all absent parents and enlist their cooperation. As new boys join the troop, you should contact their parents and present the camping story. Make sure parents of new boys receive camp literature and reservation cards.

# Suggested Agenda for Parents' Night on Camping

**Preopening.** Activity. Boy leadership. 5 minutes.

**Opening.** Ceremony. Boy leadership. 5 minutes.

**Remarks.** Introductory statement by the troop committee chairman. 5 minutes.

**Presentation.** Movie, video, or color slide presentation on the summer camp. 30 minutes.

**Boy's View.** A day in camp with the troop. Described by one of the boy leaders. 5 minutes.

**Report.** Report on troop activities by a troop outdoors/activity committee member. 10 minutes.

**Report.** Troop finance/records member explains fees. 5 minutes.

**Clinching it.** By the troop leader. 15 minutes.

**Literature.** Distribution of camp folders and other information. Troop committee outdoor/activity member. 10 minutes.

**Closing.** Ceremony. Boy leadership. 5 minutes.

# Transportation for Tours and Camps

For trips beyond hiking distance, you may need to arrange for private cars. Trucks may not be used for transporting boys except inside the cab. Insurance companies may refuse to accept responsibility if this rule is violated. These vehicles are covered as commercial haulers, but not as buses. Private cars or licensed buses should be used.

An adult leader or transportation committee member should plan for the needed cars well in advance. Go over the section on "Safe Transportation" in *Campways Tours and Expeditions*. Make certain that the condition of each car to be used is safe and each is properly insured.

General guidelines to follow: (1) All drivers must be licensed; (2) an adult leader at least 21 years of age must be in charge and accompany the trip; (3) there must be a licensed driver at least 18 years of age in each car; (4) all driving (except short trips) should be done in daylight; (5) adequate property damage and public liability insurance must be carried; (6) do not exceed limit of vehicles; and (7) do not travel in convoy.

**Tour Permits.** Your council keeps a record of all trips and tours to your council camps, areas ordinarily used by troops of the council for short-term camping, and all other destinations within 250 miles from the homes of your troop members and inside the continental United States. A local tour permit should be obtained from the local council.

If you plan a trip beyond 250 miles, you are required to submit a National Tour Permit Application, No. 4419, through your council for approval at least 1 month prior to the date of the troop's departure.

*Campways Tours and Expeditions* is recommended for planning tours. This manual and the applications have been developed to aid you in arranging for successful tours, to safeguard Scouting and its members, and to assist your council in fulfilling its responsibility for determining proper preparation before giving approval to touring groups of the council.

While on tour you must have your national tour permit in your possession and show it when requested by Scouting officials or authorized persons.

This permit is not only proof that your troop is an authorized tour group but that you have made preparations and registered with your council. It helps them know where you will be during your tour.

# Camping Honors

**National Camping Award.** Recognition is made annually to the troop that has an outstanding outdoor program. The minimum requirements for the National Camping Award are as follows:

1. Patrol Activities: Each patrol of the troop must have participated in at least three of the following activities during the last 12 months:

   • Attended camporee

   • Held a day hike

   • Completed a conservation project

   • Attended a Scout retreat

   • Conducted a Scouting Anniversary Week outdoor project

   • Conducted an approved patrol campout

   • Attended a klondike derby

2. Short-Term Camp: All patrols in the troop must have been represented in four or more short-term campouts during the past 12 months.

3. Long-Term Camp: All patrols in the troop must have been represented in a long-term (6 or more consecutive days) camp and at least 50 percent of the total boy membership of the troop attended.

These requirements will also be found in the *Troop Record Book,* along with space to record individual Scout participation in patrol and troop hikes, short-term camps, camporees, long-term camp, and other outdoor activities. An application for the National Camping Award is also included.

**Order of the Arrow.** This is the national brotherhood of honor campers. Its purpose is to recognize those campers who best exemplify the Scout Oath and Law in their daily lives and to develop and maintain camping traditions and spirit. The opportunity for receiving this honor is bestowed on a Scout by his fellow campers in his troop. He must prove himself worthy of receiving it by being an outstanding Scout and a good and unselfish camper.

# Conservation Projects

Conservation work, both by the troop and individual Scouts, is an integral part of the outdoor program. Scouting has always been much concerned with conservation, and this is reflected in advancement requirements.

Two of the skill awards—Conservation and Environment—require projects in learning how to conserve natural resources. Several merit badges, including one required for Eagle—Environmental Science—are also directly concerned with nature and conservation. For Star, Life, and Eagle ranks, the Scout must do a service project, which may be in the conservation field.

Your Scoutmaster may obtain guidance on conservation projects suitable for either an individual Scout or the whole troop by checking with your council, the U.S. Soil Conservation Service, fish and game agencies, and other conservation authorities. Sample projects include control of erosion in a school yard, park, or recreation area; planting trees or shrubs to help beautify the community; planting food shrubs for wildlife; building brush piles for wildlife cover; and building baths, houses, and feeders for birds.

Other problems that make good projects include elimination of roadside litter, participation in forest-fire prevention, planting of shade trees, construction of a nature trail in a local park, or preparing and giving talks on good outdoor manners.

Field trips may be made to such places as a managed watershed or forest, a wildlife management area, a stream that is improved for fishing, an industrial plant to observe water and air-pollution control methods, a water-treatment plant, or the weather bureau to see flood forecasting methods.

# Troop Equipment

Another function related to equipment and facilities is to train and counsel your troop quartermaster to check the inventory of equipment and devise means for storage and repair. The troop committee should approve purchases of new equipment. If you are assigned the responsibility for equipment, you should make recommendations to the committee on the need and kind of equipment desired. To secure the best value for money spent, you should get from several sources price quotations for consideration by the committee.

Equipment represents a large portion of troop expenditures. For this reason it is important that you and the quartermaster maintain a complete and detailed inventory on all equipment owned by the troop. An inventory form is part of the *Troop Financial Record Book.* On this form, you and the troop quartermaster should record the date every item is purchased or received, a description of the item, where it is stored, its cost or value, its disposition, as well as check marks for each inventory. Properly used, this form tells you at a glance all the pertinent facts about troop property, and you will know if needed equipment is available for any activity.

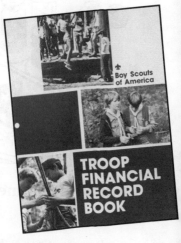

Inventory checks should be made around October 1, January 1, and May 1 of each year. If any equipment is disposed of during the year, the details should be entered in the disposition column.

Frequently, lack of equipment stands in the way of a hiking and camping troop. But that can be overcome. A new troop can often borrow or rent the tents and other equipment it needs. Meanwhile, working with your Scoutmaster, patrol leaders' council, and parents, you can devise a plan in which everyone can share in a money-earning project for obtaining equipment.

# Basic Troop Camping Equipment

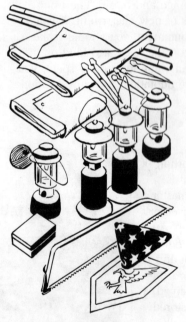

2 leaders' tents with poles and pegs

1 storage tent

1 equipment chest

4 lanterns

1 bow saw

1 first aid kit

1 ball binder twine

1 U.S. flag

1 troop flag

# Patrol Equipment

Records of patrol equipment similar to those of the troop should be kept. At regular intervals the troop quartermaster and patrol leader should make a complete updated inventory of troop property checked out to the patrol with the estimated value of each item. This list should not include just the camping equipment, but also things kept in patrol storage. The inventory should contain an evaluation of each article—is it in good condition, does it need repair to put it in working order, or should it be replaced?

After making such an inventory, you, the patrol leader, the troop quartermaster, and the treasurer should draw up a recommendation to the committee for a patrol money-earning or equipment-making program to bring the patrol gear up to the mark. (See *The Official Patrol Leader Handbook.*)

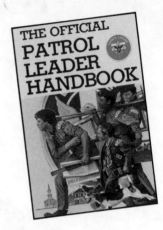

## Basic Patrol Camping Equipment

4 tents with poles and pegs
(1 tent for every two boys in patrol)

1 Scout ax

1 8-inch mill file

1 sharpening stone

1 tent repair kit

1 12 x 16-foot dining fly

1 cook kit (Trail chef or homemade)

2 plastic water bags or buckets

1 trench shovel

1 U.S. flag (small)

1 patrol flag

# Chapter 6

# FINANCE/RECORDS
## (Treasurer)

As the troop finance/records (treasurer) member, you have accepted the troop responsibility for maintaining sound financial records. You should work closely with the Scoutmaster and the troop committee chairman in discharging the following important duties:

- Handle all troop funds. Pay bills on recommendation of Scoutmaster and authorization of troop committee.

- Maintain checking and savings accounts.

- Train and supervise the troop scribe in record keeping.

- Receive troop income each week from the troop scribe.

- Keep adequate records in the *Troop Financial Record Book*, No. 6508.

- Supervise money-earning projects including obtaining proper authorization.

- Supervise the camp saving plan.

- Report to the troop committee at each meeting.

- Give leadership to the preparation of the annual troop budget.

- Have a simple annual audit of the troop finances.

# Collecting Dues and Keeping Records

Scouts must be expected to keep their dues payments up to date. They should be kept informed of their dues status, and both they and their parents should be advised of nonpayment. A Scout troop can only encourage good money practices by helping Scouts to learn to meet their obligations.

Some troops may collect dues on a monthly basis and still adhere to this system and its benefits. Annual collection of dues is not approved by the Boy Scouts of America for these reasons: (1) Annual dues are large enough to prohibit some boys from joining, and (2) Such collection usually means the parents pay the dues and the boy loses the sense of responsibility and the training that comes from paying dues weekly.

The record system described below has worked satisfactorily for a great many years in thousands of troops.

1. Before the first meeting each month, the troop scribe checks the *Troop Record Book* and prepares each Patrol's Envelope, No. 3816, with members' names and dues accounts. He confers with the Scoutmaster and distributes to patrol scribes weekly. The names of inactive Scouts are not listed.

2. The patrol scribe collects dues from its members, puts them in the envelope, and records the amount paid on the face of the envelope.

3. The troop scribe collects the patrol dues envelopes, checks the amount in each, and records the amount paid after each Scout's name in the *Troop Record Book*. At the next meeting, he returns the envelope to the patrol for reuse.

4. The scribe transmits dues to the troop treasurer in a Report to the Treasurer Envelope, No. 3851.

5. The troop treasurer posts the amount of income from dues to the *Troop Financial Record Book* and deposits the funds in the troop's bank account. The treasurer also checks the scribe's records from time to time.

6. The record is brought forward by the troop scribe and posted to a new envelope at the end of each month. The old envelope is turned over to the troop treasurer.

# Troop Bank Account With Petty Cash

You should put the troop funds in a checking account in a local bank. An account requiring two signatures on each check is recommended.

Your Scoutmaster will need a number of miscellaneous articles for the troop from time to time. Protect the Scoutmaster from the natural tendency to pay small bills, postage, etc., out of pocket.

Establish a petty cash account in the amount of $10 or $20 for the Scoutmaster. When most of this fund has been paid out, the Scoutmaster accounts for it with the receipts for purchases and secures a new advance from the treasurer. This procedure eliminates a great deal of lost motion. Larger bills are paid by the treasurer upon recommendation of the Scoutmaster and with the approval of the troop committee at a regular committee meeting.

# Camp Savings Plan

No Scout need miss summer camp because of cost. A systematic savings plan will ensure the Scouts in your troop of a long-term camp experience. A member of the troop committee or some other adult should coordinate this effort. By October 1, the camp savings plan material should be explained to boys and parents.

Personal Savings Record Cards, No. 3654, are available in quantity from the council service center. The card is in two sections: one section is kept by the Scout, the other is retained by the troop.

Encourage Scouts to deposit money at weekly meetings toward their fee. Scouts who have most of their fee on deposit by spring usually are able to get the balance and thus attend camp.

Successful camping troops vigorously promote the camp savings plan. Encourage your Scouts to earn their own funds for summer camp. Suggested projects are:

- Troop-sponsored dinners

- Paper drives

- Collecting aluminum cans for recycling

- Cooperative car wash

- Baby-sitting service

- Lawn care service

- Paper routes

Encourage parents and relatives to give their Scout sons a week at camp or partial camp fee for a birthday gift, Christmas present, or other special recognition.

# The Budget Plan

Businesslike finance management not only assures that the troop will remain solvent and have what it needs; it also provides a fine example for Scouts.

A good troop should neither run on the brink of insolvency nor accumulate surpluses. It should neither spend more than it earns nor earn more than it spends. As much harm can be done with one extreme as with the other.

Therefore, troop finances must be budgeted. The following steps are taken in preparing the total budget:

## Preparing the Budget

A budget is a plan for receiving and spending money. A troop budget is made up a year at a time, usually for the year covered by the troop charter, though it may be based on a calendar or program year.

In developing the budget, expenses for the year must be estimated and a plan devised for meeting those expenses.

To determine what the troop expenses will be for the year, the troop annual program must be analyzed. Past expenses will serve as a guide for judging amounts needed for each budget category.

In keeping with the principles of Scouting, the program of the troop is paid for by the members with money they earn and save themselves. A troop that operates through the generosity of others and finances itself by the efforts of adults fails in its responsibility to teach Scouts self-reliance.

The three general sources of budget support are dues paid by Scouts, unexpended balance from previous budgets, and troop money-earning projects.

The dues paid by Scouts should cover some basic unit expense items, such as: registration fee, *Boys' Life* magazine, advancement awards, and insignia of membership and office. In this way the boy "pays his own way." Larger or capital expenses are covered through money-earning projects that the Scouts take part in.

The following steps are taken in preparing the total budget:

- A rough draft of the budget is prepared by the Scoutmaster, troop treasurer, and troop scribe. This is a pencil draft, subject to change.

- The patrol leaders' council carefully reviews the rough draft of the budget and puts it into final form.

- The troop committee gives final approval to the budget and assumes the responsibility for the next step.

- The parents and Scouts are informed about the budget so that all will understand the individual Scout's responsibility in making it work. See *Troop Financial Record Book,* No. 6508.

## Basic Expenses

*Unit Charter Fee.* All units are required to pay an annual charter fee of $20. This fee shall be submitted with the unit's charter application and will help defray the expenses for the general liability insurance program. These fees will raise approximately 25 percent of the funds required to maintain insurance coverage for all chartered organizations and leaders.

*Registration.* When a boy joins, normally the troop asks him to pay the full $7 national registration fee regardless of the number of months remaining in the troop's charter year. The troop sends to the council the pro rata amount for those remaining months. Note that fees are figured on a monthly basis: 35¢ a month or $7 a year.

The balance of the boy's fee is kept in the troop treasury to supplement his dues in paying the next full year's fee. This procedure ensures prompt registration at charter renewal time.

*Boys' Life. Boys' Life* magazine, the official publication of the Boy Scouts of America, is available to all members at $6.60, or half the regular rate. Every boy should subscribe to *Boys' Life* because of the quality reading and the articles related to your unit's monthly program. It is part of a boy's growth in Scouting, too, and research proves he will stay in longer and advance farther if he reads *Boys' Life.*

If the reserve funds will allow, the new boy, during the charter year, should be signed up for *Boys' Life* on a pro rata basis. When reserve funds do not pay for the subscription, then the boy or his parents may be asked for the amount. They should understand that the *Boys' Life* subscription cost is not a required part of the national membership fee.

*Unit Accident Insurance.* Each unit should be covered by unit accident insurance to help meet the costs of medical care if accidents occur. The insurance fees listed are subject to adjustment.

*Reserve Fund.* The reserve fund might be established by a gift or loan from the chartered organization, members of the committee, or by a unit money-earning project. The reserve fund should meet unexpected expenses that occur before dues are collected or other money is earned. A new member's initial expenses may be met from the fund.

A small portion of each boy's expenses is budgeted to maintain this fund. If the reserve fund falls below this amount, it should be restored through a money-earning project or other means.

*Other Basic Expenses.* These expenses include insignia of membership and rank for each boy to ensure prompt recognition and literature required by unit adult and boy leaders. Because service to others is fundamental in Scouting, the budget should include a goodwill project, Good Turn, or a gift to the World Friendship Fund.

**Other Expenses**

*Program Materials.* Each unit needs to provide a certain amount of program materials. For example, it should have United States and unit flags and equipment and supplies for its regular program.

*Activities.* The size of the budgeted amount for activities depends on the unit program. Usually, such activities as Cub Scout pinewood derbies and Boy Scout hikes, camping, or Varsity Scout high-adventure trips are financed by the boy and his family over and above the dues program.

As a special note, refreshments at parties or parents' meetings can be homemade or met by a cover charge or "kitty" at the event. Regular unit funds should not be used for this purpose.

## Sources of Income

*Dues.* The finance plan of any unit should include participation by a boy in a regular dues plan. An annual unit fee, too often completely contributed by parents, does little to teach a boy responsibility. However, if he has to set aside a little each week for a desired item, such as dues, he learns how to budget his own income.

Paying dues regularly is not easy, but it does help develop character in an individual boy. It teaches responsibility and a wholesome attitude toward earning his own way.

The weekly or monthly dues envelopes for Boy Scout patrols provide a handy means of recording dues for boys who pay on a regular basis, catch up on back dues, or pay in advance. If a boy is behind in dues, adult leaders should find out why. Adult leaders may also help provide a solution through individual work projects.

In some units, boys earn their dues by participating in unit money-earning projects. It is important that such work be credited to the boy personally rather than to the unit as a whole so he will develop a sense of personal responsibility and participation.

Regardless of your dues collection plan, or how many months or weeks they are collected, individual dues should cover the basic expenses totaling $18.30 as shown in the recommended budget. You may also want dues to cover a part of the program and activity budget.

*Money-Earning Projects.* A well-rounded unit program requires supplemental income. It might come from the sale of a product or a project involving the talents, participation, or efforts of the unit members or families. Policies and procedures are in the financial record books for troops.

Most projects require the submission of the Unit Money-Earning Application, No. 4427, to the local council service center. To ensure conformity with all Scouting standards on money earning, leaders should be familiar with the 10 guides listed on the back of the application and in the financial record books.

## 10 Tests for Unit Money-Earning Projects

Here are some guides to help you determine whether your project conforms to Scouting standards for money earning.

**1.** Have your troop committee, chartered organization, and local council approved your project, including the dates and methods?

**2.** Do your plan and the dates avoid competition with money-raising programs and policies of your chartered organization, local council, community chest, or United Way?

**3.** Is your plan in harmony with local ordinances, free from any stigma of gambling, and consistent with the ideals and the purposes of the Boy Scouts of America?

**4.** If a commercial product is to be sold, will it be on its own merits and without reference to the needs of Scouting either directly (during sales presentation) or indirectly?

**5.** If tickets are sold for any function other than a Scouting event, will they be sold by your boys as individuals without depending on the goodwill of Scouting to make the sale possible?

**6.** When sales are confined to parents and immediate friends, will they get their money's worth from any product they purchase, function they attend, or services they receive from your unit?

7. If a project is planned for a particular area, do you respect the rights of other Scouting units in the same neighborhood?

8. Is it reasonably certain that people who need work or business will not lose it as a result of your troop's plan?

9. Will your plan protect the name and goodwill of the Boy Scouts of America and prevent it from being capitalized on by promoters of shows, benefits, or sales campaigns?

10. If any contracts are signed by your troop, will they be signed by an individual without reference to the Boy Scouts of America and in no way appear to bind the local council or the Boy Scouts of America to any agreement of financial responsibility?

**Other Helps**

Additional information concerning unit budget plans, the treasurer's job, camp savings, forms, and records is in *Troop Financial Record Book,* No. 6508; Unit Budget Plan, No. 28-426.

# Budget Work Sheet

To develop your unit budget, complete, with the unit leader, the work sheet below, then have it adopted by the unit committee. The patrol leaders' council reviews the budget and puts it in final form prior to study and adoption by the troop committee. Be sure to keep parents informed.

## Expected Income for Year

Number of meetings _____

Amount of dues each meeting                    $_____

Annual dues per member
    (dues × number of meetings)         $_____

Average membership in a year _____

Total dues per year
    (annual dues × average
    membership)                                       $_____

Other income

_____    $_____

_____    $_____

_____    $_____

Total other income                                      $_____

Total budgeted income
    (total dues + total other income)      $_____


## Budgeted Expenses for Year

| | |
|---|---|
| Registration | $    7.00 |
| *Boys' Life* | 6.60 |
| Accident Insurance | 1.20 |
| Reserve fund | 1.00 |
| Other basic expenses (badges, literature, goodwill) | 5.50 |
|     a. Total per boy | $   21.30 |

b. Average yearly
    membership _____

Total basic expenses (items a × b)        $_____

Unit charter fee                                       $   20.00

Program materials                                   $_____

Activities                                                 $_____

Total budgeted expenses
    (total basic expenses + program
    materials + activities)                        $_____

# Chapter 7

# ADVANCEMENT

Scout advancement is one of the eight methods we use to motivate and direct a boy's growth. Each step in the advancement plan is designed to help the boy on the road to maturity and participating citizenship. As an advancement committee member, you are responsible for the following:

- Encourage all Scouts to advance in rank.

- Promote First Class emphasis in the troop.

- Arrange monthly troop boards of review.

- Conduct Star-Life boards of review.

- Arrange for Eagle Scout board of review.

- Advise Tenderfoot-First Class boards of review.

- Conduct courts of honor following boards of review.

- Develop and maintain merit badge counselor list.

- Make prompt report on advancement report to council service center following each troop board of review.

- Secure badges and certificates.

- Work with Scoutmaster (or assistant) and troop scribe in maintenance of all Scout advancement records.

- Work with librarian in building and maintaining a troop library of merit badge pamphlets.

# Purpose of Advancement

The real purpose of advancement in Scouting is defined as follows:

*The Boy Scout advancement plan is designed to encourage Scouts to accomplish a progressive series of learning experiences in the areas of citizenship, character, and personal fitness. It provides for recognizing and measuring these experiences. Thus, we are not merely teaching particular skills such as how to live com-*

fortably in camp or how to handle emergency first aid treatment. Important as these skills may be, our real purpose is to help the boy grow—in citizenship, character, and personal fitness—and to recognize his growth. Each step in the advancement plan should have learning outcomes bearing on that purpose.

# How a Boy Scout Advances

A Boy Scout advances by taking part in activities with his patrol and troop and by doing things on his own. The troop committee and other leaders are responsible for providing opportunities for a Scout to advance.

There are four steps to advancement: The Scout learns; he is tested; he is reviewed; and he receives the award.

**Learning.** A Boy Scout learns by doing. He learns outdoor skills by hiking and camping. He learns Scout skills in patrol and troop sessions. He advances naturally by doing things with his fellow Scouts.

The Boy Scout learns with the help of his patrol leader, other patrol members, leadership corps members, merit badge counselors, Scoutmaster, and other instructors. You are responsible for finding the specialized help needed for more technical projects and for securing merit badge counselors for subjects desired and needed by your Scouts in their quest for advancement and personal growth.

The Boy Scout also learns by improving his own ability as he teaches others some of the skills and shares some of the knowledge he has been acquiring. For merit badges, a Scout works directly with the merit badge counselor. He discusses the merit badge subject with the counselor who is an adult selected because of character, interest in youth, and special skill in the subject. Then he carries out the projects that he and the counselor have discussed—with the counselor serving as his coach. As a Scout completes the projects on his own, he is learning by doing.

**Testing.** To pass his requirements for a skill award, a Scout demonstrates his ability to his patrol leader, leadership corps member, or other qualified boy leader. In some instances, it may be necessary for an adult leader in the troop to serve as counselor for a skill award when boy leaders may not be qualified in the subject.

Convenient "scoreboards" for each stage of a Scout's advancement are located in the back of his copy of *The Official Boy Scout Handbook*. As he meets a requirement for a skill award or rank, the leader who tested him signs his book.

A patrol leader may test a Scout on his advancement requirements by planning a patrol hike that involves an advancement requirement. Frequently, the Scout passes the test without realizing he is being tested. This type of practice should be a natural part of the patrol and troop program until testing, like learning, becomes the natural result of Scouting experiences.

To pass requirements for a merit badge, the merit badge counselor will certify the completion of the requirements on a merit badge application.

The testing process places challenging projects before a boy. As he prepares to meet advancement requirements, the boy develops confidence by learning that he can meet the challenge.

**Scoutmaster Conferences.** One of the most enjoyable experiences of being a Scoutmaster is the opportunity for a Scout and his leader to sit down and visit together.

In large troops, Scoutmasters may assign this responsibility to assistant Scoutmasters or members of the troop committee. This is unfortunate, because most Scoutmasters feel that this is truly the opportunity to get to know the Scout and help him chart his course in life.

A good conference should be unhurried and private. It helps the Scout evaluate his accomplishments and to set new goals with his Scoutmaster. This is a rare opportunity for a one-on-one relationship, and can be accomplished at a troop meeting, camping trip, or in the home.

Goal setting by the Scout makes it possible for the Scoutmaster to encourage the Scout to use his strengths and to help him with his weaknesses.

The Scout joining conference is probably one of the most important associations the boy will have in his Scouting career. It is at this conference that the Scoutmaster illustrates to him the adult-youth relationship that is unique to Scouting.

All through the ranks, it is rewarding for the Scoutmaster to observe the Scout grow in responsibility and maturity. It is through this association and example that a boy grows and matures, and the Scoutmaster conference accomplishes that aim.

A unit of training, *Scoutmaster Conference*, No. 6560A, is available for instruction in how to conduct these conferences.

**Reviewing.** The board of review—the final step before the Scout receives his badge—has three objectives:

1. Determining the extent to which the Scout has had an effective experience in the troop.

2. Making certain that advancement standards have been met.

68

**3.** Encouraging the Scout to progress further.

The patrol leaders' council has the responsibility for conducting boards of review for Tenderfoot, Second Class, or First Class. The senior patrol leader or his appointee is chairman of the board of review. The reviewers, a group of the Scout's peers, are members of the patrol leaders' council. They should question the Scout and judge his readiness for advancement.

A member of the troop committee serves as adviser to the patrol leaders' council board of review for the first three ranks. The committee member should be an adviser, not the chief reviewer. A portion of the adviser's responsibility is to evaluate how well the patrol leaders' council members conduct this review. The adviser usually does not participate in questioning the Scout, but must assure that standards are maintained.

For Star, Life, and Eagle Palms the board of review is conducted by the troop committee. The Eagle board of review may be conducted on a troop, district, or council level. Your local council determines which method or methods are used. If conducted on a troop level, a member of the council or district committee responsible for advancement serves as a member of the review board.

**Awarding the Badge.** The Scout should receive his badge without delay. Skill awards should be presented as soon as they have been earned—at the troop meeting or during a troop activity. Merit badges and ranks should be awarded within a week to 10 days after they have been earned. The closing portion of a troop meeting is a good time for this recognition.

A formal troop court of honor should be held at least four times a year, and Scouts who have already received awards at troop meetings are then publicly recognized. The responsibility for setting up courts of honor and securing awards is shared by the troop committee and patrol leaders' council.

# Conducting the Board of Review

The following suggestions for conducting a board of review apply to the patrol leaders' council as well as troop committee members.

**Preliminaries.** Before any review, discuss with the patrol leader or Scoutmaster the boys to be reviewed. They can brief you so you are prepared to handle each individual. Review one boy at a time. This gives the boy special attention. Furthermore, if a troop meeting is going on, it doesn't disrupt the meeting by having many boys absent.

The boy's patrol leader, senior patrol leader, or Scoutmaster should accompany the boy into the room and introduce him to the members of the board of review. As members of the review board, you should help the Scout feel at ease. Invite him to be seated and talk about his patrol or other matters of interest to him. At first, ask questions you know he will be able to answer. This informal period assures the boy he is among friends.

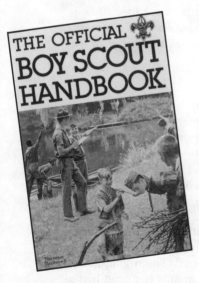

**The Board of Review.** The reviewers must satisfy themselves that a satisfactory standard has been maintained. Use *The Official Boy Scout Handbook* or the *Boy Scout Requirements* book as a guide for the requirements of each rank. Avoid using a set formula or list of questions. Questions should determine that each individual boy has met the standards. The review should be as much a part of the educational experience as learning and testing.

The following questions are merely a guide to the kind of questions that might be asked.

*On Scout Activity:* Have you taken part recently in any service projects? How many members of your patrol or leadership corps were with you? What did you do? Would you like to do it again? How do you think this helped other people? What is the name of your patrol, and how many members are in it? Has your patrol taken part in outdoor activities? Did you have a chance to cook as a patrol? If you did, how did you work together?

*On Skill Awards and Merit Badges Required for Rank Advancement:* Note the requirements the boy has met. Question him to satisfy yourself that he knows what the requirements demand. For example: How would you orient a map? What would you do if you met a man bleeding profusely? How do you pitch a tent properly?

The purpose is not to reexamine the Scout on every point of the requirements, but to determine that he has a practical working knowledge of the required material.

*On Scout Ideals:* The requirements are intangible, and specifics are hard to pin down. You should be looking for understanding and awareness rather than concrete evidence. For example: What do you mean when you say "On my honor I will do my best"? (Expect a boyish answer, which, nevertheless, can reveal whether the Scout has a basic understanding of what he is promising to do.) Do you do a Good Turn every day? (Be prepared for a "no" answer, but do not use this as a basis for turning the boy down. The purpose of the question is to alert the boy to the pledge he has made and thus increase his effort to fulfill it.) How do you keep yourself physically strong? (More specific answers may be expected in this instance.)

Your questions should have one fundamental objective—good standards of performance. Boys should not get the notion that your review is merely a rubber-stamp approval. On the other hand they should not feel that it is a rigid, formal checkup.

*On Service Projects:* Review the Scout on the service he has performed. For the first three ranks, the Scout should be able to describe enough Good Turns to show you that he thinks about doing Good Turns regularly.

For the Star and Life ranks, the Scout must take part in clearly defined, approved service projects. For Eagle, he must plan, develop, and give leadership to others in a successful service project for a religious institution, school, or home community. The project must be approved in advance by the Scoutmaster and troop committee and by the district or council committee responsible for advancement.

*On Religious Principles:* The following guides may help the board of review in areas related to religion:

- The Boy Scouts of America expects a member to subscribe to religious principles stated in the *Bylaws of the Boy Scouts of America,* in the Scout Oath and Law, and on the application for membership. This involves the following commitments: duty to God, reverence toward God, fulfillment of religious duties, respect for the convictions of others.

- The Boy Scouts of America has reaffirmed its conviction of "duty to God" in the Scout Oath and Law but feels that the interpretation and definition of God should be in the hands of families and religious leaders.

- The Boy Scouts of America strongly encourages its members to participate in the religious programs and activities of a church, synagogue, mosque, or other religious organization.

- The religious institutions of America commend the Boy Scouts of America for encouraging its members to participate in organized religious activities.

If a Boy Scout says he is a member of a particular religious body, he must be evaluated by the standards of the group to which he belongs. This is why for the Eagle Scout rank, reference is usually requested from his religious leader who will indicate whether, in his estimation, the Scout lives up to his expectations. In most instances, the reviewers will discover that the Scout belongs to some religious group and his participation can be readily determined.

There are those who do not believe that it is necessary to subscribe to an organized form of religion. They seek to practice religion in accord with their own personal convictions. The reviewers should make an effort to understand, through discussion with the Scout, his religious convictions and standards in order to determine whether he has fulfilled his religious duties. If it becomes apparent that a determination cannot be made without a discussion with the Scout's parents, the adviser to the board of review should take over the responsibility for final action. The adviser should, in conjunction with the Scoutmaster and the troop committee, arrange for a meeting with the parents and the Scout to reach a conclusion.

**The Board of Review Decision.** At the conclusion of the review, you should know whether a boy is qualified for the rank award. Discuss whether he measures up while he waits in another room. When you call him back, congratulate him if he has done well and encourage him to achieve further skills and recognition in Scouting.

When a boy is not ready for advancement, give him the opportunity to face up to himself. Praise him on as many points as possible, then ask him whether, considering his entire performance, he thinks his advancement should be approved. In most cases, he will know that he is not prepared.

Your considerate handling of the boy at this critical moment can go far in establishing a more positive approach to future projects. Advise the boy that he will be given every help to prepare himself for a board of review in the near future. Boys respect adults and Scouts who demand high standards. Notify the Scoutmaster immediately of your decision and why. As each boy is approved, enter his name on the Advancement Report, No. 4403, which must be submitted to the council service center.

An important function of the review is to review Scouts who are not advancing. When a boy does not advance the reviewers have a responsibility to learn why and to stimulate him to do so. The process also shows you where the troop can put emphasis to improve its program.

For the greatest effect, the board of review should be held on a specified date each month. A practical plan is to hold the review at the same time the troop meets or at the monthly patrol leaders' council meeting. If possible, use a room adjoining the meeting place.

# Courts of Honor

Each time a Boy Scout advances in rank, he should be recognized on two occasions. The first should occur as soon as possible after a Scout has been approved by a board of review and the advancement report has been submitted to the local council—preferably at the next unit meeting. This ceremony should be dignified but simple, involving not much more than presenting the Scout with his new badge of rank.

The second occasion is a formal court of honor, a public ceremony to recognize Scouts for successful achievement and to describe the importance of the program. The main purposes of the court of honor are to furnish formal recognition for achievement and to provide incentive for other Scouts to advance.

Formal courts of honor should be conducted at least four times a year. All Scouts who have advanced since the previous court of honor are honored. Their parents and friends should be invited to attend the ceremony.

When a Scout has earned the Eagle Award, he deserves a special recognition. The award ceremony may not be conducted until the action of the board of review has been approved by the National Council.

# Service Projects

**Star and Life Ranks.** For Star
and Life ranks, a Scout must perform 6 hours of service to
others. This may be done as an
individual project or as a member of a patrol or troop project.
Star and Life service projects
may be approved for Scouts
assisting on Eagle service
projects. The Scoutmaster
approves the project before it is
started.

**Eagle Rank.** To qualify for the
Eagle service project while a Life
Scout, a boy must plan, develop,
and give leadership to others in
a service project to a religious
institution, school, or community.
These projects, of course, must
conform to the wishes and regulations of those for whom the
project is undertaken.

As a demonstration of leadership, the Scout must plan the
work, organize the personnel needed, and direct the project to its
completion.

Service to others is important. Work involving council
property or other BSA activities is not acceptable for an Eagle
service project. The service project also may not be performed for
a business or be of a commercial nature or be a fundraiser.

Routine labor, a job or service normally rendered, should not be considered. An Eagle service project should be of significant magnitude to be special. Total amount of time involved must be considerable and should represent the candidate's best possible effort.

In order to ensure that the service project for Eagle is noteworthy, the Scout must secure the prior approval of his unit leader and unit committee. The project must be reviewed and approved by the district or council advancement committee or their designee to make sure that it meets the stated standards for Eagle Scout service projects before the project is started. This preapproval of the project does not mean that the board of review will accept the way the project was carried out.

Upon completion of the project, a detailed report must be submitted with the Scout's Eagle application to include the following information:

- What was the project?

- How did it benefit others?

- Who from the group benefiting from the project gave guidance?

- Who helped carry out the project?

- What materials were used and how were they acquired?

Although the project idea must be approved before work is begun, the board of review must determine if the project was successfully carried out. Questions that must be answered are:

- Did the candidate demonstrate leadership of others?

- Did he indeed direct the project rather than do all of the work himself?

- Was the project of real value to the religious institution, school, or community group?

- Who from the group benefiting from the project may be contacted to verify the value of the project?

- Did the project follow the plan or were modifications needed to bring it to its completion?

All the work on the project must be done while the candidate is a Life Scout and before the candidate's 18th birthday, unless a time extension has been granted by the national Boy Scout Committee.

The Eagle service project is an individual matter; therefore, two Eagle candidates may not receive credit for the same project.

The variety of good projects performed throughout the nation by Scouts earning their Eagle Award is staggering. Only those living in an area can determine the greatest value and need. Determine, therefore: Is the project big enough, appropriate, and worth doing? For ideas and opportunities, the Scout can consult people such as school administrators, religious leaders, local government department directors, or a United Way agency's personnel.

The district advancement committee also can be helpful by identifying possible projects.

# The Merit Badge Program

The purpose of the merit badge program is to provide:

- Opportunities for Boy Scouts to plan and carry out projects toward their own growth and development

- Opportunities for Scouts to learn about many subjects including Scout skills, career, hobby, cultural, and service fields

- Enough orientation in these fields to serve as a springboard for further exploration and to help a Scout discover his talents

- Useful skills in many subjects leading toward capable, participating citizenship

- Involvement in activities of interest to boys

More than 100 merit badge subjects and pamphlets are available. Scouts choose the ones they wish to explore. Scouts may work on merit badges on their own or in groups with a merit badge counselor. Some merit badges such as Camping and Cooking are most likely to be earned as a natural result of patrol and troop activity.

When the Scout determines he is ready to work for a merit badge, he discusses available merit badge counselors with the Scoutmaster who helps him select one. The Scoutmaster then signs the merit badge application that the Scout will present to the merit badge counselor. The Scoutmaster tells the Scout that there is a pamphlet on every merit badge.

**The Merit Badge Counselor.** The merit badge method is unique. It is based on a counselor working closely with the Scout. This acquaints a boy with a new adult, an expert in one or more fields, who introduces him to subjects that are often of career or hobby value.

In addition to technical knowledge, the counselor must have an understanding of boys and be sympathetic with their interests and abilities. The counselor must be a person of unquestionable character. All merit badge counselors must be approved by the council advancement committee and registered as adult members of the BSA.

**The Counseling Procedure.** When a Scout has obtained his Scoutmaster's approval to begin working on a merit badge, he makes an appointment with the counselor for that badge. This usually results in a series of conferences as the counselor advises and coaches the Scout. During the first meeting the counselor should discuss the requirements and projects with the Scout. As the Scout works to complete these requirements and projects, the counselor gives him guidance and may teach him basic techniques. The counselor really functions as a coach.

The Scout is expected to meet the requirements as stated—no more and no less. Furthermore, he is to do exactly what is stated. If it says "show or demonstrate," that is what he must do. Just telling about it isn't enough. The same thing holds true for such words as "make," "list," "in the field," and "collect, identify, and label."

When a boy feels he is qualified, his counselor reviews him on what he has learned and his completed projects. When satisfied that the Scout is qualified, the counselor signs the application. There are three parts to this application: the applicant's record, the counselor's record, and the approval portion with the signatures of the counselor and Scoutmaster. The Scout gives this approval portion to the Scoutmaster for submission to the council on the advancement report. The Scout should receive his badge and certificate at the next troop meeting following submission of the advancement report. This recognition signifies genuine accomplishment.

**Merit Badge Counselor Lists.** Your district and/or council will have a list of approved merit badge counselors from which your troop can draw. Your troop will build up and maintain a list of approved counselors, drawing from the parents of the Scouts, troop leaders, committee members, former Scouts, members of the chartered organization, and other people in the neighborhood. All merit badge counselors must be approved by the council advancement committee. They may register as Scouters, but this is not required. The opportunity to recruit parents of Scouts as counselors should be stressed, particularly in one-troop communities.

Merit Badge Counselor Information Sheet, No. 4405, is used to enroll merit badge counselors and determine their qualifications in a particular subject. Work sheet for Building a Merit Badge Counselor List, No. 4436, will be helpful in making a list of your troop merit badge counselors.

## Advancement in Camp

Summer camp offers an ideal situation for a boy to learn skills, qualify for advancement, and be recognized. Councils have a responsibility to provide the necessary personnel and equipment and adequate opportunities for boys to participate in the advancement program while at Scout camp. Every summer camp should have a procedure for Scout advancement that takes into account all four processes of advancement: learning, being tested, being reviewed, and receiving the award. All the necessary report forms and cards should be at camp, and the program director of the camp should have recognition materials.

# Special Recognitions

There are additional special opportunity awards available to Scouts in such areas as outdoor activities, aquatics, conservation, and religion. Further information may be obtained from *The Official Boy Scout Handbook, Boy Scout Requirements,* or by making an inquiry at your local council service center.

# Learning Your Job

Those related to advancement on the troop committee must become thoroughly familiar with the Boy Scout advancement plan. You can do this by reading, by personal conferences with district leaders or members of the council advancement committee, or by taking the training provided by the district or council. In addition, roundtable programs often feature advancement.

Your goal should be to make advancement available to all boys. Your minimum troop program should have every new Boy Scout advance to First Class in his first year and at least one rank each year thereafter. Boy Scouts who are not advancing should be reviewed to find out why.

The Boy Scout advancement plan is limited to registered Boy Scouts, Varsity Scouts, and Explorers through age 17. For more information on advancement procedures for the handicapped, see *Advancement Guidelines,* No. 3087A, or contact your local council service center.

# Chapter 8

# HEALTH
# AND SAFETY

Health through knowledge and safety through skill are fundamental ideas behind all Scout activities. Therefore, take the initiative to ensure health and safety measures, including:

- Arrange medical health history/examinations.

- Supervise meeting place inspections for safety.

- Secure tour permits.

- Be responsible for an insurance program.

- Promote good health and safety conditions in meeting place and at sites used for outdoor activities.

- Coordinate first aid, aquatics, and safety program resources.

# Medical Health History/Examination

The health and physical fitness of each troop member should be a primary interest. A current health history (updated each year at charter renewal time) should be on file and shared with the troop leadership. Conditions such as diabetes, asthma, epilepsy, or allergies should be discussed with parents for medications and care in the event signs or symptoms occur. Family physicians should be known in the event that parents are not readily available during a medical emergency. The health history form on the back of the membership application is normally sufficient to alert your adult leadership of any conditions that they need to be aware of.

The Boy Scouts of America recommends that all members have periodic medical evaluation by a physician. It is required that Boy Scouts, participating in any activity over 72 consecutive hours where the activity is similar to that normally expended at home or school and emergency medical care is readily available (within the hour), have a medical evaluation (physical examination) conducted by a physician within the past 36 months. *The Personal Health and Medical Record, Class 2,* No. 4414, available from the BSA is recommended to obtain necessary medical data on each Boy Scout.

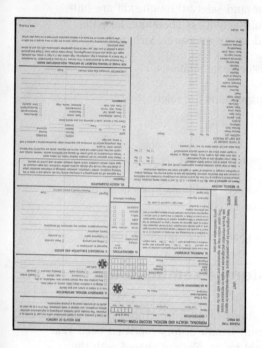

*The Personal Health and Medical Record, Class 3,* No. 4412A, must have been completed by a physician within the last 12 months in situations where Scouts are exposed to strenuous activity such as backpacking, high altitude, extreme weather conditions, cold water (70° or lower), exposure, fatigue, athletic competition and/or remote conditions where emergency medical care is not readily available (over an hour response time).

Frequently, you may find a physician in your neighborhood or community who would be willing to conduct these medical evaluations for the members of your troop prior to the long-term summer camping experience at little, or no expense, to your Scouts. It never hurts to inquire. Perhaps a parent of one of your Scouts is a physician.

# Meeting Place Inspections

Periodically, at least once a year, inspect the facilities where the troop meets for health conditions and possible hazards.

The BSA has a checklist entitled Meeting Place Inspection, No. 6140, available through your local council. Use your Scouts to help conduct this inspection. If conditions are found unsatisfactory, your Scouting coordinator should be advised for further action. If the troop could help correct the situation, this should also be cleared in advance.

This might be a good opportunity to do a fire drill, or discuss what actions would need to take place in the event of an emergency occurring during a troop meeting (i.e., tornado, heart attack, explosion, etc.) Develop procedures to fit your location.

# First Aid Training and Equipment

At least one member of your adult leadership team should have a minimum of Standard American Red Cross First Aid training, and it would be advisable if every adult had this training. If enough people are interested (including parents), make arrangements through your local Red Cross chapter to have a course conducted where your troop meets.

A container of first aid supplies should be gathered for (1) your troop meeting room, *and* (2) troop activities away from your regular meeting site. It should be your responsibility to determine what needs to be included in these containers, and to keep them stocked. Adhesive bandages and antiseptics tend to disappear quickly.

# Health and Accident Insurance

**Unit Accident Insurance Plan.** Unit accident insurance is available through your local council. Information is sent to troops each year in their charter renewal kit, and the coverage must be applied for by the troop. This plan provides coverage for accident medical expenses and accidental death and dismemberment while participating in any approved and supervised Scouting activity, including going to and from meetings. New members are automatically covered under the plan until renewal date. Non-Scouts attending scheduled activities for the purpose of being encouraged to participate in Scouting are also automatically covered.

**A Council Accident and Sickness Insurance Plan.** This is provided for youth and adult members registered in the council, and covers them for accidents and sickness (as well as accidental death and dismemberment) while participating in any official Scouting activity.

**Camper's Accident and Sickness Insurance Plan.** This plan is provided for all youth and adults registered in the council and all other persons registered and attending official council events (i.e., summer camp, day camps, Wood Badge courses, etc.). It is purchased for specific events of the council and provides coverage for medical expenses for accidents and sickness and accidental death and dismemberment.

**Comprehensive General Liability Insurance.** This coverage provides protection for the council; all Scouting officials, directors, officers, and professional and nonprofessional employees; and currently registered Scouting units, their chartered organizations, and volunteer Scouters (whether or not registered) with respect to liability claims arising out of negligence in the performance of their duties in Scouting.

This insurance does not take the place of any volunteer's personal liability insurance under a homeowners or automobile liability insurance policy, nor does it provide medical payments for injuries. BSA coverage is excess over other valid and collectible insurance carried by volunteers. Chartered organizations, however, are provided primary coverage as respects liability arising out of their sponsorship of any Scouting activity.

**Automobile Liability Insurance.** Every person who drives a car in connection with a Scouting activity should carry a minimum of $50,000/$100,000/$25,000 of automobile liability limits on their vehicle. A tour permit or a council short-term camping permit is required when units leave their immediate area. National tour permits are required for all trips more than 500 miles. These permits should list the drivers' names and limits of automobile liability insurance carried.

# BSA Guidelines on Troop Programs, Tours, and Activities

Over the years, the BSA has developed policies, standards, and guidelines applicable to the galaxy of activities in which Scouts may become involved. These have been developed to create an awareness of possible hazards and reduce the possibility of serious injury or even death.

Most of these policies and standards are published in the literature of the BSA. To help you become familiar with what they are and where they can be found in detail, the *Health and Safety Guide*, No. 4409, is available as a resource. The contents of this guide includes information on aquatics, camping, cycling, drug abuse, emergency service, fire prevention, first aid, firearms, hazardous activities, inspections, medical information, serious or fatal injuries or illnesses, transportation, trail safety, and winter activities.

Still another publication that would be good to share with your troop leadership is *Tours and Expeditions*. It covers recommendations for troop planning any type of short- or long-term activity that takes the group out onto the highway for any extended period of time.

Your awareness of these guidelines, and your bringing them to the attention of your troop leadership as the occasion arises, may well prevent an unhappy ending to what could have been an exciting adventure for the Scouts and leadership of your troop.

# Chapter 9

# SERVICE/GOOD TURN

- Stimulate community Good Turns and service projects.

- Serve as counselor for advancement service projects.

- Approve Eagle Scout service projects.

- Promote an emergency service plan.

- Encourage personal Good Turns.

- Promote service projects for chartered organization.

**Service Program for the Troop.** The service program of the troop should be planned in such a way that it will tie in with other programs being conducted in the community. Study the local situation and find out where the troop's services will do the most good and what the boys are best qualified to do.

It is important that Scouts be involved in finding, selecting, and planning the service project. This is a job for the patrol leaders' council. Make sure every Scout gets a chance to suggest troop service projects.

**Periodic Service.** Find annual recurring opportunities for service projects, such as the following:

- Collection of old clothing, or toys for repair

- Assist chartered organization (sponsor) with annual event

- Observance of state and national holidays

- Aid to social or charitable organizations

- Participation in United Way campaign

**Occasional Service.** Call institutions and organizations to help with specific needs and services, such as:

- Messengers, guides, or ushers for public meetings

- Distribution of posters or literature for community organizations

- Duty at community gathering or school athletic events

- Assistance in safety drives, cleanup campaigns, and other community projects

- Cooperation with rescue squad in locating lost children

- Assistance at church or community functions as ushers or special helpers

**Emergency Service.** Boy Scout service is invaluable in time of emergency or calamity—flood, fire, explosion, windstorm, or other disaster. Scout training should result in preparedness to render assistance in rescues, life saving, first aid, signaling, messenger service, cooking, and camping.

The troop should have a mobilization plan, by which the Scouts and troop equipment can be quickly assembled. Test the efficiency of the mobilization organization at least annually. It should be more than a mere paper plan.

# Daily Good Turn

The Good Turn is the surest way of helping a boy realize that he is a part of a great country and to develop the habit of thinking of other people. Encourage the patrol leaders' council to make this a regular part of the troop program.

# Chapter 10

# TROOP CHAPLAIN

In this capacity, you as the chaplain have an opportunity to be a friend to the Scouts and leaders, and contribute to their spiritual welfare and growth. You as the chaplain, by virtue of your position and personality, can encourage the boys in their Scouting work and other aspects of their total lives. Your responsibilities are:

- Provide a spiritual tone for troop meetings and activities.

- Give guidance to the chaplain aide.

- Promote regular participation of each member in the activities of the religion of his choice.

- Visit homes of Scouts in time of sickness or need.

- Give spiritual counseling service when needed or requested.

- Encourage Boy Scouts to earn their appropriate religious emblem.

- Provide opportunities for Boy Scouts to understand their "duty to God."

- At boards of review and other occasions, such as Scoutmaster's Minutes, challenge Scouts to think about their "duty to God."

# Outreach Opportunities

Many times one of the first contacts a new family has in the community is with the Scouting unit. As new members are registered, you will learn of their religious affiliations or interest. Extend an invitation to join in worship with you, or share with them the opportunities within the community. At no time should the chaplain proselytize.

# Accidents, Illnesses, and Other Problems

Ask the leaders to report accidents, illnesses, and other problems of members to you. You should become aware of situations where a pastoral call would be appropriate and beneficial. Leaders who are in regular contact with their members often are the first to know of situations that may need pastoral attention.

If a member misses several meetings, it may be an indication that something is wrong. Ask that the names of absentees be shared with you. As chaplain you have the opportunity of visiting and discovering the source of the problem. If the problem is with some aspect of the Scouting program or leadership, you should discuss this problem with the appropriate individual or committee.

## Scouting Coordinator

This person is the representative of the chartered organization to the district and local council. This person must be able to represent the organization's concern in both policy making and program. The chaplain should work closely with the Scouting coordinator for the interest of the chartered organization and its ministry, and concern for children, youth, and families.

## Support of Unit Leadership

Unit leaders are charged with fulfilling the purpose of both the chartered organization and Scouting. The leadership should demonstrate awareness of an understanding of both. It should be evident that Scouting activities are fulfilling spiritual needs, as well as developing Scouting skills.

## Religious Emblems Study Programs

Encourage Scouts to earn their appropriate religious emblems. The troop may be composed of Scouts of various faiths, therefore a knowledge of all programs would be helpful. The pamphlet Religious Emblems Quick Reference Chart, No. 5-206A, will be most helpful. Procedures within various denominations differ. A call to your local council service center will help to identify the requirement book, method of ordering, and presentation.

## Chaplain Aide

A chaplain aide is an approved youth leadership position for Boy Scouts. His responsibilities are to encourage spiritual awareness and growth in the lives of troop members and to assist the chaplain.

## Sensitivity to Needs

Working with leaders and youth will offer you an opportunity to relate to them at a level where you will become sensitive to needs not yet expressed. Be alert for personal, family, or social situations that may require special care.

# Chapter 11

# SUSTAINING MEMBERSHIP ENROLLMENT CHAIRMAN

As SME enrollment chairman you are responsible for conducting the enrollment in your troop and inviting all its families to become sustaining members, this includes the following:

- Participate in the orientation meeting.

- Enroll as sustaining member.

- Select, train, and enroll needed personnel to conduct the troop's enrollment.

- Attend district kickoff meeting.

- Follow up until all cards are accounted for.

- Conduct report meetings.

- Give recognition to contributors and enrollers.

- Work closely with public relations person (secretary).

The local council provides many services to make possible the Scouting program for your troop. These services include program, support materials, training, advancement program, activities, camping facilities, high-adventure opportunities, and personnel readily available to assist in making possible a better program for your troop.

Sustaining membership enrollment (Friends of Scouting in some councils) is a primary source of operating income for the council. Sustaining members are those individuals with an interest in the Boy Scouts of America and a desire to financially support the program. When properly informed and given the opportunity, many families of youth members wish to become sustaining members.

Each troop is encouraged to select a person to be responsible for enrolling families as sustaining members. The enrollment normally takes place in one of two methods. In some troops, the troop sustaining membership enrollment chairman selects other parents to personally visit families and provide them an opportunity to become sustaining members. Other troops will conduct a presentation during a parents' night program, Scouting anniversary dinner, or court of honor. Following the presentation, families are given the opportunity to enroll as sustaining members.

The amount of a family membership is determined by the council. Some councils arrive at a cost per youth member and others have a fixed family membership.

# Chapter 12

# PARENTS

## Parents' Auxiliary in the Unit

Parents of youth members are members of the parents' auxiliary.

Activities affecting youth members and unit leaders should be planned with leaders and the unit committee.

Purposes:

- To provide support for youth members and unit leaders

- To provide a support group for parents

Suggested activities arranged by the parents' auxiliary:

- Scouting Anniversary Week event

- Court of honor party

- Old-timers' night

- Welcoming new parents

- Picnics

- Block party

- Fundraising event

- Social event for leaders of chartered organization

# Suggested Letter to New Parents

To the Parents of our Newest Member,

We are pleased to welcome your son as a member of the Boy Scouts of America. This membership makes you a Scout parent and your family a Scout family. We hope you will all enjoy and benefit from this association.

We intend to help you develop your son into a man who is physically strong, mentally awake, and morally straight.

It's exciting and beautiful to watch a life develop and know you are being part of it. We feel that a child must grow from the early stage of complete dependence on his family to an eventual state of self-dependence. Along the line he must be given increasing opportunity to make responsible decisions and to try himself out in many situations. This development begins with tight family control that must gradually change to family support.

You can use our program to help you guide your son in this developmental process. We will support your moral values and religious preferences. Here are ways you can use the Scouting program to help your son develop and grow:

- Encourage your Scout to have perfect attendance at all troop meetings and activities.

- Be interested in and encourage advancement.

- Provide some suitable way for your Scout to earn dues money or make it a part of an allowance for which he is still to fulfill his responsibilities to his family.

- If possible, as he matures, have him earn money for the troop campouts.

- Encourage him to pay his dues regularly as part of his learning the responsibility of handling money and his responsibility to his troop finances.

- Attend all troop courts of honor, if possible.

- Aid in providing transportation for troop activities.

Best wishes to you as you move into the exciting experience of helping your son develop and grow. Make it a happy time, a warm time, a time when you both discover each other. And let Scouting help you. Use it to enrich your son's life.

Sincerely,

# Chapter 13

# POLICIES
# AND PRINCIPLES

As a troop committee member you advise the Scoutmaster on the purposes and principles of the Boy Scouts of America and your chartered organization. To do so you must become familiar with these policies and enforce their observance.

## Religion

The Boy Scouts of America maintains that no member can grow into the best kind of citizen without recognizing an obligation to God. In the first part of the Scout Oath or Promise the member declares, "On my honor I will do my best to do my duty to God and my country and to obey the Scout Law." The recognition of God as the ruling and leading power in the universe and the grateful acknowledgment of His favors and blessings are necessary to the best type of citizenship and are wholesome precepts in the education of the growing members. No matter what the religious faith of the member may be, this fundamental need of good citizenship should be kept before him. The Boy Scouts of America therefore recognizes the religious element in the training of the member, but it is absolutely nonsectarian in its attitude toward that religious training. Its policy is that the home and the organization or group with which the member is connected shall give definite attention to religious life.

Only persons willing to subscribe to this declaration of principle shall be entitled to certificates of leadership in carrying out the Scouting program.

The activities of the members of the Boy Scouts of America shall be carried on under conditions which show respect for the convictions of others in matters of custom and religion, as required by the twelfth point of the Scout Law, reading "Reverent. A Scout is reverent toward God. He is faithful in his religious duties. He respects the beliefs of others."

In no case where a unit is connected with a church or other distinctively religious institution shall boys of other denominations or faith be required, because of their membership in the unit, to take part in or observe a religious ceremony distinctly peculiar to that institution or church.

# Commercialism

No troop may enter into a contract or business relationship that can be construed as using the Scouting movement for commercial purposes, such as an effort to capitalize on public interest in the Scouting movement rather than depending upon the merits of the business proposition. This shall not be interpreted, however, as interfering with any Scout earning money for his own Scouting equipment or for his troop, provided the money is earned through service actually rendered and is not dependent upon capitalizing on interest in the Boy Scouts of America.

Your troop may conduct a money-earning project only when the project has been approved by the council and when it is consistent with this statement on commercialism. Guidelines for money-earning projects are detailed in the discussion of finances of the troop.

Your council may approve the public sale of tickets to such Scouting activities as merit badge shows, circuses, rallies, and demonstrations provided that the nature of the program offers a value commensurate with the price of the ticket, the ticket sale is not used as an indirect method for defeating the purpose of this statement on commercialism, and that the Scout's participation in the ticket sale is confined to his parents and immediate friends and does not involve methods similar to those used in the sale of tags and other solicitations.

Local authorities may make arrangements for Scouts to cooperate with well-established nonpartisan and nonsectarian national movements for the relief of humanity in certain undertakings to raise money. Limit such cooperation to giving personal service; do not involve the use of Scouts as solicitors of money.

Scouts may cooperate in civic and other public gatherings of a nonpartisan and nonpolitical character in a way which gives Scouts an opportunity to render service in harmony with their training in Scouting instead of merely taking part in parades or making a show of themselves.

# Troop-Owned Property

The Boy Scouts of America discourages troops from building or developing permanent cabin or camp facilities for these reasons: The limited use of such facilities does not justify the required expense. Such a camp tends to discourage the use of varied campsites. Cabins and permanent buildings used year-round for camping purposes do not support the camping aims and ideals of Scouting. Boys learn little about camping when all they have to do is open a door and throw their blankets on the bed. Vandalism is a threat. Such camps usually come into disuse after 2 years with resulting rapid deterioration.

Troop-owned campsites and facilities can be a financial burden due to cost of insurance, maintenance and replacement of equipment, and losses because of vandals.

## Smoking and Drinking

The Boy Scouts of America recommends that intoxicating liquors not be used in connection with any Scout meetings, and that all Scoutmasters and other officials while on active duty refrain from the use of tobacco. Those who are accustomed to the use of tobacco should not conceal the fact from the boys, but should discuss frankly with them the desirability of refraining from its use.

# Competition

The Boy Scouts of America believes competition should be used as a vital learning process, a means of enhancing the growth and development of boys. Three kinds of competition are recognized.

1. Group competition with overall winners. Patrols or troops may compete against each other in events in a rally, camporee, etc. Points are given to the winners, and troops or patrols winning the most points win the overall event.

2. Group competition to a standard. Groups such as patrols demonstrate their skill and are given points according to a rating plan. There is no individual winner, but each group is encouraged to attain the highest possible rating.

3. Individual competition. Certain events in a competitive activity might, by their very nature, be designed for individual competition. In such cases there are, of course, individual winners, but such winners also should win points for their patrol or troop as a contribution to the total effort.

One of the methods for meeting boys' interest in competition will be by the use of team sports on an informal basis and as a natural part of troop activities. Contact sports that involve heavy physical contact should not be used in this program. Such sports cannot be safely conducted without proper equipment, special facilities, constant conditioning, and trained coaches.

# Uniforming

The troop committee should encourage the uniforming of the troop. The Boy Scout uniform is part of the romance of Scouting. A boy's uniform, with badges to show his awards, gives him pride in his appearance. It helps him to feel that he belongs, that he is truly a member of a great world brotherhood. The uniform puts all Scouts on the same level.

However, the troop committee should keep in mind the following:

- Many boys may not be able to afford a uniform right away. Earning and saving is the recommended method of obtaining a uniform.

- Money earned by the boys individually may be matched with money earned through troop and patrol projects.

- The troop committee should cooperate with the Scoutmaster in developing opportunities whereby members of the troop can earn money to secure the uniform.

## Hazing

Older Scouts sometimes feel that new Scouts should be initiated into the troop with a hazing activity. Hazing has no place in Scouting.

## Wilderness Policy of the Boy Scouts of America

All private or publicly owned backcountry land and designated wilderness are included in the term "wilderness areas" in this policy. The Outdoor Code of the Boy Scouts of America applies to outdoor behavior generally, but for treks into wilderness areas minimum impact camping methods must be used. Within the outdoor program of the Boy Scouts of America, there are many different camping skill levels. Camping practices that are appropriate for day outings, long-term Scout camp, or short-term unit camping do not apply to wilderness areas. Scouts and Explorers need to adopt attitudes and patterns of behavior, wherever they go, that respect the rights of others, including future generations, to enjoy the outdoors.

In wilderness areas, it is crucial to minimize our impact on particularly fragile ecosystems such as mountains, lakes, streams, deserts, and seashores. Since our impact varies from one season of the year to the next, it becomes important for us to adjust to these changing conditions to avoid damaging the environment.

The Boy Scouts of America emphasizes these practices for all troops, teams, and posts planning to use wilderness areas:

- Contact the landowner or land managing agency (Forest Service, National Park Service, Bureau of Land Management, U.S. Fish and Wildlife Service, State, private, etc.) well in advance of the outing to learn the regulations for that area and to obtain required permits and current maps.

- Always obtain a tour permit, available through local council service centers, meet all conditions specified, and carry it on the trip.

- Limit the size of groups generally to no more than 8 to 11 persons, including at least one adult leader (maximum: 10 persons per leader). Two leaders per group are best. Do not exceed the group size if one has been established for the wilderness area. Organize each group (patrol, team, or crew) to function independently by planning their own trips on different dates, serving their own food, providing their own transportation to trailhead, securing individual permits, and camping in a separate and distinct group. When necessary to combine transportation and planning or buying, small groups should still camp and travel on the trail separately from other groups of the same unit.

- Match the ruggedness of high-adventure experiences to the skills, physical ability, and maturity of those taking part. Save rugged treks for older youth members who are proficient and experienced in outdoor skills.

- Participate in training for adult leaders in low-impact camping or be proficient and experienced in the leadership and skills required for treks into wilderness areas.

- Conduct pretrip training for the group that stresses proper wilderness behavior, rules, and skills for all of the potential conditions that may be encountered.

- Use backpacking stoves, particularly where the fuel supply is limited or open fires are restricted. Supervision by an adult knowledgeable in the use of the stoves must be provided. If a fire is necessary, keep it as small as possible and use established fire lays where available if in a safe area. After use, erase all signs.

- Emphasize the need for minimizing impact on the land through proper camping practices and preserving the solitude and quietness of remote areas. Camp in low-use areas—avoid popular sites that show signs of heavy use.

- Leave dogs, radios, and tape players at home.

- Use biodegradable (not metal or glass) or plastic food containers. Carry out unburnable trash of your own and any left by others.

- Dig shallow holes for latrines and locate them at least 200 feet from the nearest water source. Cover the latrines completely before leaving.

- Wash clothes, dishes, and bodies at least 200 feet from source of natural water.

- Where a choice is available, select equipment of muted colors that blend with natural surroundings.

- Look at and photograph; never pick or collect.

- Follow trail switchbacks and stay on established trails.

- Treat wildlife with respect and take precautions to avoid dangerous encounters with wildlife. Leave snakes, bears, ground squirrels, and other wildlife alone.

# UNIT COMMISSIONER

Name _____

Address _____ ZIP _____

Phone: (H) _____ (B) _____


# DISTRICT COMMISSIONER

Name _____

Address _____ ZIP _____

Phone: (H) _____ (B) _____


# DISTRICT EXECUTIVE

Name _____

Address _____ ZIP _____

Phone: (H) _____ (B) _____

# TROOP COMMITTEE HOW-TO BOOK

The Troop Committee How-To Book is a pullout section designed to be pulled out of the *Troop Committee Guidebook*. Each page contains an individual troop committee member's responsibilities and should be given to that member as a quick reference on what is expected.

# TROOP COMMITTEE RESPONSIBILITIES

## WHAT Does the Troop Committee Organization Do?

- Provide adequate meeting facilities.

- Advise Scoutmaster on policies relating to the Boy Scout program and the chartered organization.

- Carry out the policies and regulations of the Boy Scouts of America.

- Encourage leaders in carrying out the Boy Scout program.

- Be responsible for finances, adequate funds, and disbursements in line with the approved budget plan.

- Obtain, maintain, and care properly for troop property.

- Provide adequate camping and outdoor program (minimum 10 days and nights per year).

- See that adult leadership is assigned in case the Scoutmaster is absent or is unable to serve.

- Operate troop to ensure permanency.

Duplicate this page for each member of the troop committee.

# DUTIES OF TROOP COMMITTEE MEMBERS

Each member of the committee should have specific responsibilities, thus dividing the whole job among the membership to carry out the pledge made at the time of the application for charter.

*Note of caution:* Exercise care to see that in no instance do committee members encroach upon the rightful responsibilities of the Scoutmaster or assistants.

# CHAIRMAN

Name _____

Address _____ ZIP _____

Phone: (H) _____ (B) _____

- Organize the committee to see that all functions are delegated, coordinated, and completed.

- Maintain a close relationship with the Scouting coordinator.

- See that leadership and committee have training opportunities.

- Interpret national and local council policies to troop.

- Work closely with Scoutmaster in preparation of agenda for troop committee meeting.

- Call, preside, and promote attendance at monthly troop committee meetings and any special meetings that may be called.

- Ensure troop representation at monthly roundtables.

- Secure topflight, trained individuals for camp leadership.

- Arrange for charter review and recharter the troop annually.

# TROOP COMMITTEE RESPONSIBILITIES

## WHAT Does the Troop Committee Organization Do?

- Provide adequate meeting facilities.

- Advise Scoutmaster on policies relating to the Boy Scout program and the chartered organization.

- Carry out the policies and regulations of the Boy Scouts of America.

- Encourage leaders in carrying out the Boy Scout program.

- Be responsible for finances, adequate funds, and disbursements in line with the approved budget plan.

- Obtain, maintain, and care properly for troop property.

- Provide adequate camping and outdoor program (minimum 10 days and nights per year).

- See that adult leadership is assigned in case the Scoutmaster is absent or is unable to serve.

- Operate troop to ensure permanency.

Duplicate this page for each member of the troop committee.

# DUTIES OF TROOP COMMITTEE MEMBERS

Each member of the committee should have specific responsibilities, thus dividing the whole job among the membership to carry out the pledge made at the time of the application for charter.

*Note of caution:* Exercise care to see that in no instance do committee members encroach upon the rightful responsibilities of the Scoutmaster or assistants.

# MEMBERSHIP/
# RELATIONSHIPS
## (Secretary)

Name _____

Address _____ ZIP _____

Phone: (H) _____ (B) _____

- Keep minutes of meetings and send out committee meeting notices.

- Handle publicity.

- Conduct parent orientation for new families.

- Prepare family newsletter of troop events and activities.

- Work with troop historian.

- Assist in annual membership inventory and inspection program.

- Arrange for proper welcome of Webelos Scouts graduating into troop.

- Invite all Webelos Scout families to assist with troop program.

- Conduct boy-fact survey and troop resource survey.

- Plan for family night programs and family activities.

- See that the troop sets membership goals and adopts and carries out a troop recruiting plan.

- Plan charter presentation program.

# TROOP COMMITTEE RESPONSIBILITIES

**WHAT Does the Troop Committee Organization Do?**

• Provide adequate meeting facilities.

• Advise Scoutmaster on policies relating to the Boy Scout program and the chartered organization.

• Carry out the policies and regulations of the Boy Scouts of America.

• Encourage leaders in carrying out the Boy Scout program.

• Be responsible for finances, adequate funds, and disbursements in line with the approved budget plan.

• Obtain, maintain, and care properly for troop property.

• Provide adequate camping and outdoor program (minimum 10 days and nights per year).

• See that adult leadership is assigned in case the Scoutmaster is absent or is unable to serve.

• Operate troop to ensure permanency.

Duplicate this page for each member of the troop committee.

# DUTIES OF TROOP COMMITTEE MEMBERS

Each member of the committee should have specific responsibilities, thus dividing the whole job among the membership to carry out the pledge made at the time of the application for charter.

*Note of caution:* Exercise care to see that in no instance do committee members encroach upon the rightful responsibilities of the Scoutmaster or assistants.

# OUTDOOR/ACTIVITIES

Name _____

Address _____ ZIP _____

Phone: (H) _____ (B) _____

- Supervise and help procure camp equipment.

- Work with Scoutmaster or assistant and quartermaster on inventory, storage, and proper maintenance of troop equipment.

- Help in securing permission to use camping sites.

- Serve as transportation coordinator.

- Encourage monthly outdoor activities or special activities.

- Promote National Camping Award and Fair Way camp promotion plan.

- Promote—through family meetings—attendance at troop camps, camporees, and summer Scout camp to reach the goal of 10 days and nights of camping for each Scout.

- Coordinate family camping program.

# TROOP COMMITTEE RESPONSIBILITIES

**WHAT Does the Troop Committee Organization Do?**

- Provide adequate meeting facilities.

- Advise Scoutmaster on policies relating to the Boy Scout program and the chartered organization.

- Carry out the policies and regulations of the Boy Scouts of America.

- Encourage leaders in carrying out the Boy Scout program.

- Be responsible for finances, adequate funds, and disbursements in line with the approved budget plan.

- Obtain, maintain, and care properly for troop property.

- Provide adequate camping and outdoor program (minimum 10 days and nights per year).

- See that adult leadership is assigned in case the Scoutmaster is absent or is unable to serve.

- Operate troop to ensure permanency.

Duplicate this page for each member of the troop committee.

## DUTIES OF TROOP COMMITTEE MEMBERS

Each member of the committee should have specific responsibilities, thus dividing the whole job among the membership to carry out the pledge made at the time of the application for charter.

*Note of caution:* Exercise care to see that in no instance do committee members encroach upon the rightful responsibilities of the Scoutmaster or assistants.

# HEALTH AND SAFETY

Name _____

Address _____ ZIP _____

Phone: (H) _____ (B) _____

- Arrange physical examinations for entire troop.

- Supervise meeting place inspections for safety.

- Secure tour permits.

- Be responsible for insurance program.

- Promote good health and safety conditions in meeting place and at sites used for outdoor activities.

- Coordinate first aid, aquatics, and safety program resources.

# TROOP COMMITTEE RESPONSIBILITIES

**WHAT Does the Troop Committee Organization Do?**

- Provide adequate meeting facilities.

- Advise Scoutmaster on policies relating to the Boy Scout program and the chartered organization.

- Carry out the policies and regulations of the Boy Scouts of America.

- Encourage leaders in carrying out the Boy Scout program.

- Be responsible for finances, adequate funds, and disbursements in line with the approved budget plan.

- Obtain, maintain, and care properly for troop property.

- Provide adequate camping and outdoor program (minimum 10 days and nights per year).

- See that adult leadership is assigned in case the Scoutmaster is absent or is unable to serve.

- Operate troop to ensure permanency.

Duplicate this page for each member of the troop committee.

# DUTIES OF TROOP COMMITTEE MEMBERS

Each member of the committee should have specific responsibilities, thus dividing the whole job among the membership to carry out the pledge made at the time of the application for charter.

*Note of caution:* Exercise care to see that in no instance do committee members encroach upon the rightful responsibilities of the Scoutmaster or assistants.

# FINANCE/RECORDS
## (Treasurer)

Name _____

Address _____ ZIP _____

Phone: (H) _____ (B) _____

- Handle all troop funds. Pay bills on recommendation of Scoutmaster and authorization of troop committee.

- Maintain checking and savings accounts.

- Train and supervise the troop scribe in record keeping.

- Receive troop income each week from the troop scribe.

- Keep adequate records in the *Troop Financial Record Book*, No. 6508.

- Supervise money-earning projects including obtaining proper authorization.

- Supervise the camp savings plan.

- Report to the troop committee at each meeting.

- Give leadership to the preparation of the annual troop budget.

- Have a simple annual audit of troop finances.

# TROOP COMMITTEE RESPONSIBILITIES

## WHAT Does the Troop Committee Organization Do?

- Provide adequate meeting facilities.

- Advise Scoutmaster on policies relating to the Boy Scout program and the chartered organization.

- Carry out the policies and regulations of the Boy Scouts of America.

- Encourage leaders in carrying out the Boy Scout program.

- Be responsible for finances, adequate funds, and disbursements in line with the approved budget plan.

- Obtain, maintain, and care properly for troop property.

- Provide adequate camping and outdoor program (minimum 10 days and nights per year).

- See that adult leadership is assigned in case the Scoutmaster is absent or is unable to serve.

- Operate troop to ensure permanency.

Duplicate this page for each member of the troop committee.

# DUTIES OF TROOP COMMITTEE MEMBERS

Each member of the committee should have specific responsibilities, thus dividing the whole job among the membership to carry out the pledge made at the time of the application for charter.

*Note of caution:* Exercise care to see that in no instance do committee members encroach upon the rightful responsibilities of the Scoutmaster or assistants.

# ADVANCEMENT

Name _____

Address _____ ZIP _____

Phone: (H) _____ (B) _____

- Check to see that Scouts advance in rank.

- Arrange monthly troop boards of review.

- Conduct Star-Eagle boards of review.

- Advise Tenderfoot-First Class boards of review.

- Conduct frequent courts of honor, at least quarterly.

- Develop and maintain merit badge counselor list.

- Make prompt report on correct form to council service center when troop board of review is held. Secure badges and certificates.

- Work with Scoutmaster or assistant and troop scribe in maintenance of all Scout advancement records.

- Work with librarian in building and maintaining a troop library of merit badge pamphlets.

# TROOP COMMITTEE RESPONSIBILITIES

**WHAT Does the Troop Committee Organization Do?**

- Provide adequate meeting facilities.

- Advise Scoutmaster on policies relating to the Boy Scout program and the chartered organization.

- Carry out the policies and regulations of the Boy Scouts of America.

- Encourage leaders in carrying out the Boy Scout program.

- Be responsible for finances, adequate funds, and disbursements in line with the approved budget plan.

- Obtain, maintain, and care properly for troop property.

- Provide adequate camping and outdoor program (minimum 10 days and nights per year).

- See that adult leadership is assigned in case the Scoutmaster is absent or is unable to serve.

- Operate troop to ensure permanency.

Duplicate this page for each member of the troop committee.

# DUTIES OF TROOP COMMITTEE MEMBERS

Each member of the committee should have specific responsibilities, thus dividing the whole job among the membership to carry out the pledge made at the time of the application for charter.

*Note of caution:* Exercise care to see that in no instance do committee members encroach upon the rightful responsibilities of the Scoutmaster or assistants.

# SERVICE/GOOD TURN

Name _____

Address _____ ZIP _____

Phone: (H) _____ (B) _____

- Stimulate community Good Turns and service projects.

- Serve as counselor for advancement service projects.

- Approve Eagle Scout service projects.

- Promote emergency service plan.

- Promote service projects for chartered organization.

# TROOP COMMITTEE RESPONSIBILITIES

## WHAT Does the Troop Committee Organization Do?

- Provide adequate meeting facilities.

- Advise Scoutmaster on policies relating to the Boy Scout program and the chartered organization.

- Carry out the policies and regulations of the Boy Scouts of America.

- Encourage leaders in carrying out the Boy Scout program.

- Be responsible for finances, adequate funds, and disbursements in line with the approved budget plan.

- Obtain, maintain, and care properly for troop property.

- Provide adequate camping and outdoor program (minimum 10 days and nights per year).

- See that adult leadership is assigned in case the Scoutmaster is absent or is unable to serve.

- Operate troop to ensure permanency.

Duplicate this page for each member of the troop committee.

# DUTIES OF TROOP COMMITTEE MEMBERS

Each member of the committee should have specific responsibilities, thus dividing the whole job among the membership to carry out the pledge made at the time of the application for charter.

*Note of caution:* Exercise care to see that in no instance do committee members encroach upon the rightful responsibilities of the Scoutmaster or assistants.

# TROOP CHAPLAIN

- Provide a spiritual tone for troop meetings and activities.

- Give guidance to chaplain aide.

- Promote regular participation of each member in the activities of the religious organization of his choice.

- Visit homes of Scouts in time of sickness or need.

- Give spiritual counseling service when needed or requested.

- Encourage Boy Scouts to earn their appropriate religious emblem.

- Provide opportunities for Boy Scouts to grow in their relationship to God and their fellow Scouts.

# TROOP COMMITTEE RESPONSIBILITIES

## WHAT Does the Troop Committee Organization Do?

• Provide adequate meeting facilities.

• Advise Scoutmaster on policies relating to the Boy Scout program and the chartered organization.

• Carry out the policies and regulations of the Boy Scouts of America.

• Encourage leaders in carrying out the Boy Scout program.

• Be responsible for finances, adequate funds, and disbursements in line with the approved budget plan.

• Obtain, maintain, and care properly for troop property.

• Provide adequate camping and outdoor program (minimum 10 days and nights per year).

• See that adult leadership is assigned in case the Scoutmaster is absent or is unable to serve.

• Operate troop to ensure permanency.

Duplicate this page for each member of the troop committee.

# DUTIES OF TROOP COMMITTEE MEMBERS

Each member of the committee should have specific responsibilities, thus dividing the whole job among the membership to carry out the pledge made at the time of the application for charter.

*Note of caution:* Exercise care to see that in no instance do committee members encroach upon the rightful responsibilities of the Scoutmaster or assistants.

# SUSTAINING MEMBERSHIP ENROLLMENT CHAIRMAN

- Build organization to enroll parents and Scouters in the troop.

- Enroll as sustaining member.

- Recruit one person as enroller for every five families in the troop.

- Attend kickoff meeting.

- Enroll each enroller as sustaining member.

- Train enrollers.

- Conduct report meetings.

- Follow up until all cards are accounted for.

- Give recognition to contributors and enrollers.

- Work closely with the membership/relationships person.

# TROOP COMMITTEE RESPONSIBILITIES

**WHAT Does the Troop Committee Organization Do?**

• Provide adequate meeting facilities.

• Advise Scoutmaster on policies relating to the Boy Scout program and the chartered organization.

• Carry out the policies and regulations of the Boy Scouts of America.

• Encourage leaders in carrying out the Boy Scout program.

• Be responsible for finances, adequate funds, and disbursements in line with the approved budget plan.

• Obtain, maintain, and care properly for troop property.

• Provide adequate camping and outdoor program (minimum 10 days and nights per year).

• See that adult leadership is assigned in case the Scoutmaster is absent or is unable to serve.

• Operate troop to ensure permanency.

Duplicate this page for each member of the troop committee.

# DUTIES OF TROOP COMMITTEE MEMBERS

Each member of the committee should have specific responsibilities, thus dividing the whole job among the membership to carry out the pledge made at the time of the application for charter.

*Note of caution:* Exercise care to see that in no instance do committee members encroach upon the rightful responsibilities of the Scoutmaster or assistants.

# DUTIES OF TROOP LEADERS

Troop leaders lead by helping each Scout help himself. They identify each Scout's characteristics and habits in order to understand him and help him feel they have his welfare at heart. They encourage each Scout in troop activities and lead through their own example—by living the Scout Oath and Law as expected of the Scouts.

# TROOP COMMITTEE RESPONSIBILITIES

**WHAT Does the Troop Committee Organization Do?**

- Provide adequate meeting facilities.

- Advise Scoutmaster on policies relating to the Boy Scout program and the chartered organization.

- Carry out the policies and regulations of the Boy Scouts of America.

- Encourage leaders in carrying out the Boy Scout program.

- Be responsible for finances, adequate funds, and disbursements in line with the approved budget plan.

- Obtain, maintain, and care properly for troop property.

- Provide adequate camping and outdoor program (minimum 10 days and nights per year).

- See that adult leadership is assigned in case the Scoutmaster is absent or is unable to serve.

- Operate troop to ensure permanency.

Duplicate this page for each member of the troop committee.

# DUTIES OF TROOP COMMITTEE MEMBERS

Each member of the committee should have specific responsibilities, thus dividing the whole job among the membership to carry out the pledge made at the time of the application for charter.

*Note of caution:* Exercise care to see that in no instance do committee members encroach upon the rightful responsibilities of the Scoutmaster or assistants.

# SCOUTMASTER

Name _____

Address _____ ZIP _____

Phone: (H) _____ (B) _____

- Train and guide boy leaders to run **their** troop.

- Work with and through responsible adults to give Scouting to boys.

- Help boys to grow by encouraging them to learn for themselves.

- Guide boys in planning the troop program.

# TROOP COMMITTEE RESPONSIBILITIES

## WHAT Does the Troop Committee Organization Do?

• Provide adequate meeting facilities.

• Advise Scoutmaster on policies relating to the Boy Scout program and the chartered organization.

• Carry out the policies and regulations of the Boy Scouts of America.

• Encourage leaders in carrying out the Boy Scout program.

• Be responsible for finances, adequate funds, and disbursements in line with the approved budget plan.

• Obtain, maintain, and care properly for troop property.

• Provide adequate camping and outdoor program (minimum 10 days and nights per year).

• See that adult leadership is assigned in case the Scoutmaster is absent or is unable to serve.

• Operate troop to ensure permanency.

Duplicate this page for each member of the troop committee.

# DUTIES OF TROOP
# COMMITTEE MEMBERS

Each member of the committee should have specific responsibilities, thus dividing the whole job among the membership to carry out the pledge made at the time of the application for charter.

*Note of caution:* Exercise care to see that in no instance do committee members encroach upon the rightful responsibilities of the Scoutmaster or assistants.

# ASSISTANT SCOUTMASTER
## (Activities)

Name _____

Address _____ ZIP _____

Phone: (H) _____ (B) _____

- Serve as the troop leader in the absence of the Scoutmaster.

- Be responsible to the Scoutmaster for program and activities of the troop.

- Work with the assistant senior patrol leader.

- Coordinate joint Webelos den-troop activities.

# TROOP COMMITTEE RESPONSIBILITIES

**WHAT Does the Troop Committee Organization Do?**

- Provide adequate meeting facilities.

- Advise Scoutmaster on policies relating to the Boy Scout program and the chartered organization.

- Carry out the policies and regulations of the Boy Scouts of America.

- Encourage leaders in carrying out the Boy Scout program.

- Be responsible for finances, adequate funds, and disbursements in line with the approved budget plan.

- Obtain, maintain, and care properly for troop property.

- Provide adequate camping and outdoor program (minimum 10 days and nights per year).

- See that adult leadership is assigned in case the Scoutmaster is absent or is unable to serve.

- Operate troop to ensure permanency.

Duplicate this page for each member of the troop committee.

# DUTIES OF TROOP COMMITTEE MEMBERS

Each member of the committee should have specific responsibilities, thus dividing the whole job among the membership to carry out the pledge made at the time of the application for charter.

*Note of caution:* Exercise care to see that in no instance do committee members encroach upon the rightful responsibilities of the Scoutmaster or assistants.

# ASSISTANT
# SCOUTMASTER
## (Physical Arrangements)

Name _____

Address _____ ZIP _____

Phone: (H) _____ (B) _____

- Be responsible to the Scoutmaster for troop physical arrangements.

- Work with the troop quartermaster and outdoor committee member.

- Arrange for use of troop equipment by Webelos den.

- Be responsible for the care and neat appearance of all equipment.

- Be responsible for health and safety in all troop affairs.

# TROOP COMMITTEE RESPONSIBILITIES

**WHAT Does the Troop Committee Organization Do?**

- Provide adequate meeting facilities.

- Advise Scoutmaster on policies relating to the Boy Scout program and the chartered organization.

- Carry out the policies and regulations of the Boy Scouts of America.

- Encourage leaders in carrying out the Boy Scout program.

- Be responsible for finances, adequate funds, and disbursements in line with the approved budget plan.

- Obtain, maintain, and care properly for troop property.

- Provide adequate camping and outdoor program (minimum 10 days and nights per year).

- See that adult leadership is assigned in case the Scoutmaster is absent or is unable to serve.

- Operate troop to ensure permanency.

Duplicate this page for each member of the troop committee.

# DUTIES OF TROOP COMMITTEE MEMBERS

Each member of the committee should have specific responsibilities, thus dividing the whole job among the membership to carry out the pledge made at the time of the application for charter.

*Note of caution:* Exercise care to see that in no instance do committee members encroach upon the rightful responsibilities of the Scoutmaster or assistants.

# ASSISTANT SCOUTMASTER
## (Patrol Adviser)

Name _____

Address _____ ZIP _____

Phone: (H) _____ (B) _____

- Serve as adviser for a patrol or leadership corps.

- Serve as a resource person for the patrol or corps.

- Recruit others to assist.

- Support the patrol leader with advice and counseling.

When questions arise, call on persons below in order:

# TROOP COMMITTEE RESPONSIBILITIES

**WHAT Does the Troop Committee Organization Do?**

- Provide adequate meeting facilities.

- Advise Scoutmaster on policies relating to the Boy Scout program and the chartered organization.

- Carry out the policies and regulations of the Boy Scouts of America.

- Encourage leaders in carrying out the Boy Scout program.

- Be responsible for finances, adequate funds, and disbursements in line with the approved budget plan.

- Obtain, maintain, and care properly for troop property.

- Provide adequate camping and outdoor program (minimum 10 days and nights per year).

- See that adult leadership is assigned in case the Scoutmaster is absent or is unable to serve.

- Operate troop to ensure permanency.

Duplicate this page for each member of the troop committee.

# DUTIES OF TROOP COMMITTEE MEMBERS

Each member of the committee should have specific responsibilities, thus dividing the whole job among the membership to carry out the pledge made at the time of the application for charter.

*Note of caution:* Exercise care to see that in no instance do committee members encroach upon the rightful responsibilities of the Scoutmaster or assistants.

# SCOUTING COORDINATOR

Name _____

Address _____ ZIP _____

Phone: (H) _____ (B) _____

- Serve as head of "Scouting Department."

- Secure committee chairman and encourage training.

- Maintain a close liaison with troop committee chairman.

- Help recruit the right leadership.

- Serve as liaison between your units and your organization.

- Organize enough units.

- Encourage graduation of youth members from unit to unit.

- Assist with unit rechartering.

- Encourage service to organization.

- Cultivate organization leaders.

- Be an active and involved member of the district committee.

- Bring district help and promote its use.

- As a member of the local council, represent the interests of your organization.

# TROOP COMMITTEE RESPONSIBILITIES

**WHAT Does the Troop Committee Organization Do?**

- Provide adequate meeting facilities.

- Advise Scoutmaster on policies relating to the Boy Scout program and the chartered organization.

- Carry out the policies and regulations of the Boy Scouts of America.

- Encourage leaders in carrying out the Boy Scout program.

- Be responsible for finances, adequate funds, and disbursements in line with the approved budget plan.

- Obtain, maintain, and care properly for troop property.

- Provide adequate camping and outdoor program (minimum 10 days and nights per year).

- See that adult leadership is assigned in case the Scoutmaster is absent or is unable to serve.

- Operate troop to ensure permanency.

Duplicate this page for each member of the troop committee.

# DUTIES OF TROOP COMMITTEE MEMBERS

Each member of the committee should have specific responsibilities, thus dividing the whole job among the membership to carry out the pledge made at the time of the application for charter.

*Note of caution:* Exercise care to see that in no instance do committee members encroach upon the rightful responsibilities of the Scoutmaster or assistants.